Fellowship of Suffering

Peter Martin

Fellowship of Suffering

Dedication

To my parents Doug and Mary
Thank you for showing me that there is no trauma too deep that God can not heal.

Contents

Foreword
Dr. Deb Waterbury

There is always an intrinsic connection between authors. We long to relate, and we understand one another in ways others may not. Peter Martin and I definitely have that commonality, but that is certainly not where it ends.

I first met Peter when he was a guest on my radio show. I remember the day he walked into the studio, clad in basketball shorts, a T-shirt, and carrying a gallon jug of water. My guests generally came with stacks of notes and books to help them with the interview, but not Peter. He literally only carried the jug of water and nothing else. Consequently, my first thoughts went something like this: "Yikes! This is going to be a long, one-sided interview."

I couldn't have been more wrong.

Peter is an intelligent, thoughtful young man, but more than that, he truly knows his Bible. He began to speak about the passions of his heart as soon as the interview began, and he pulled biblical passage after biblical passage seemingly out of thin air throughout the course of the hour we had together. Needless to say, I was impressed. Our mutual love of writing was soon joined by our mutual love of theology.

Then Peter told me he was a U.S. Marine. My youngest son, who is the same age as Peter, is also a Marine, so I was extremely interested in his viewpoints on Post-Traumatic Stress Disorder (PTSD) and how they both affect and imprison the mental state of those returning from battle. You see, both of my sons were in the military, and both of them went to Afghanistan. In addition, my husband is a fighter pilot in the U.S. Air Force and has been to battle many times during our marriage. Consequently, the more I spoke with Peter, the more I encouraged him to write the book you have in front of you.

The effects of PTSD is an often-neglected topic, and it's most often neglected in the church. That's unfortunate, because the church is precisely where this kind of healing must begin —and end, quite frankly. Peter has lived through what most of us can only imagine, and in so doing, he is perfectly positioned to bring light to a dark subject. The light is Jesus. He's always the answer, and just because suffering of this magnitude is "handled" in mainstream psychology and psychiatry doesn't mean that the answers are there, too.

Peter examines not only the origins and exceptional pain of PTSD-related trauma in *Fellowship of Suffering*, but he goes the next necessary step toward true healing. The fact that he does so from a personal standpoint makes this book not only right on target, but it also makes it relatable in ways that few other books are. After all, as I've watched all three of my men deal on some level or another with this very debilitating mental state, I've also realized that my inability to relate makes me also unable to really help. I can love them, but that's about where my aid has to stop. None of my books, none of my counsel, and not one of the conferences I speak at will help like someone who understands will.

This is Peter's story. We all have one, and all of our stories are meant to help others find their way to healing in Christ. *Fellowship of Suffering* does precisely that, and it does it in a way that makes freedom from paralyzing trauma possible. Peter takes solid biblical truths and brings them to bear on suffering, but he does so in a particular fashion geared specifically to the hurting veteran. Whether you are that veteran or you are one who loves that veteran, these are the truths that are needed.

Everyone has a story. In order to fulfill the reason for the story and help those who will benefit from hearing it, healing must occur first. *Fellowship of Suffering* quite frankly carries the truths that will bring that healing to fruition.

Dr. Deb Waterbury is a biblical counselor and the founder of Love Everlasting Ministries, a ministry dedicated to educating and empowering women all over the world. She began the Reap What You Sew trade school (RWYS.org) for impoverished women in Malawi, Africa, and has authored fourteen books, including her most recent titles, "We are Mother Abraham" and "The Lies that Bind: And the Truth that Sets You Free." Dr. Deb travels extensively, both nationally and abroad, and hosts two weekly shows, "Real Life with Deb Waterbury" and "Get Real with Deb Waterbury." Both are available on YouTube and iTunes.

Acknowledgements

First, to God, who has saved me and shows me grace throughout my life. Without Him, I would never have found any growth or healing from my past. The hope that I write about does not come from any particular wisdom or courage from myself, but only through His grace, working through a stubborn and broken man. My strongest desire is that He would be glorified in this work and that the hope I found in Him would be yours as well.

To my wonderful and amazing wife, Emma. You have supported me in all of my work and efforts through sacrificing your time and energy to help me complete my goals, including the writing of this book. You have loved me more than I could ever deserve, and you have taught me more than I can say. Thank you for being a strong anchor for me, always pointing me toward Christ and making me a better man every day.

To my parents, Doug and Mary, who have always taught me through words and actions what it means to transform ashes into beauty through the grace and love of God, how to be better in a world that is getting worse, and the strength to remain faithful and hold a family together no matter the obstacles and challenges. Thank you for never giving up on me and loving me during my worst moments. Without you, I would have never found my way.

To my siblings, Josh, Kirsten, and Rebekah, thank you for all of your wonderful support and prayers. You have always been so loving towards me, and I can't thank you enough.

To my church, Calvary Christian Fellowship of Tucson, and especially my pastors, Beau and Scott. Thank you for discipling me, teaching me what it truly means to be a servant of God, and for remaining a strong resource for continuing my walk with God and continuing my process of healing and ministry.

Prologue
Healing Can Be Yours

"That I may know him, and the power of his resurrection, and the fellowship of his sufferings, being made conformable unto his death; If by any means I might attain unto the resurrection of the dead."
Philippians 3:10-11, NKJV

"How do you pick up the threads of an old life? How do you go on, when in your heart you begin to understand... there is no going back? There are some things that time cannot mend. Some hurts that go too deep, that have taken hold."
J.R.R. Tolkien, *The Return of the King*

In January 2010, I left the U.S. Marine Corps base at Camp Lejeune in Jacksonville, North Carolina with my unit, the Third Battalion Sixth Marines infantry regiment. We headed to Camp Leatherneck in Afghanistan to prepare to take part in what proved to be one of the largest operations in the War in Afghanistan. It was the invasion of the small, farm-oriented town of Marjah (also known as Operation Moshtarak or The Battle of Marjah) that lasted from February 13-December 7.

The operation is the focus of an excellent and accurate HBO documentary film highlighting the First Battalion Sixth Marines who arrived in Afghanistan one month before we did, and while the documentary was made about them, my unit was a full and equal part of the invasion. The First occupied the city itself while we took over a section of the outskirts of the town. Marjah was targeted because the Taliban is essentially a drug cartel, and the fields around the city were filled with poppies, the plant from which opium is derived for heroin or pharmaceutical drugs.

I was 19 years old at the time, and I felt ready and eager to fight for my country.

What I didn't understand then was that it wasn't going to be the experience itself that I was unprepared to deal with, but the aftermath.

When my unit returned to the States in August, we stayed at Camp Lejeune for a couple of weeks of combat detox, taking classes on how to reintegrate to society, before I went on leave and came home to Tucson, Arizona. After spending eight months in the chaotic, violent environment that is military combat, I tried to share my experiences with my friends from high school and my family—my parents, Doug and Mary, two sisters, Bekah and Kirsten, brother, Josh, and my Aunt Renee and Uncle Mike and their children. Yet the more I shared, the more I encountered a separation between myself and the people I loved and believed I knew so well.

Even though I felt the same, what I had been through had changed me, and I found that I was a stranger to the people I cared for the most. I had been through something they couldn't understand, and they treated me differently. They seemed nervous to be around me, and they didn't know what to say or how to respond to me. Not long after my arrival in Tucson, my aunt and uncle flew in from out of state, and we had a big family dinner at my parent's house. Everyone, especially my cousins, were conversing about their lives—and I couldn't help but feel disgusted hearing them talk about things and worrying about stuff that, to me, just didn't matter.

Not in light of what I'd just seen and experienced.

I stood up from the table right in the middle of the meal.

"Where are you going?" my mother asked.

"I'm outta here!" I replied. And I was. It was abrupt, rude, and totally out of character for me. But I just had to get away from all the idle banter.

Later, when my parents tried to press me on the matter, I got frustrated and then mad. I had this sense that I was right and that everyone else was wrong, so I pulled away.

There were other times when I'd talk about my deployment and the details of some of the firefights I was in. I described things, such as getting shot at and killing people, like they were a joke because that's how me and members of my unit talked about it when in combat. But my family and friends found it all to be disturbing, even offensive. I just thought they'd get over it. I didn't really focus on it, but it was weird. I didn't like it, and it made me pull away even more emotionally and physically.

It was simply easier to stop talking altogether.

In no time, I felt isolated and alone, even while I was trying to process and cope with what I had experienced in Afghanistan. This, in turn, filled me with emptiness and anger.

It wasn't until years later that God began to change me, and I started to become more civilized in my thinking. It was then I realized that the stuff I shared, and the way I shared it, wasn't appropriate. Only then did I try talking with my parents, but I still became noticeably upset when they mentioned anything having to do with the military. I was cold and distant. There was a disconnect between us. I didn't really feel like I belonged.

As I began working on this book, I started to more fully understand that I wasn't the only one who felt the pains of isolation created by trauma. In fact, J.R.R. Tolkien, author of *The Hobbit* and *The Lord of the Rings* trilogy, felt the same way when he came back from World War I. To help cope, he turned to writing, and at the end of his book, *The Return of the King*, Tolkien described the awkwardness of the hobbits' return home. They had gone through hell in order to save Middle-earth, and now that they were back from countless days spent in turmoil and terror, they came back to the Shire, their homeland, that was untouched by disaster. They found that the people they had fought to protect could never understand what they had been through, much less the threat they had been safeguarded from. The war-weary hobbits felt unappreciated, misjudged, and detached from everyone around them.

I read the Tolkien books, along with some other members of my unit, while we were in Afghanistan, but we had no idea Tolkien was a military veteran or of how he intentionally married the narrative and characters of the books to his experiences in combat. We thought the story was interesting, but I didn't make the connection until I started researching the accounts of other modern-day combat veterans who had learned about Tolkien and what he was communicating in his books. The film *Tolkien*, released in 2019 by Fox Searchlight Pictures and Chernin Entertainment, reveals how he and his friends were college kids, artists, and had never seen combat. Their friendship was the inspiration for the Shire. Sadly, all of them died save for Tolkien in the Battle of the Somme.

After the hobbit's long period of chaos with Merry and Pippin battling against Sauron's army while Frodo and Sam scaled Mount Doom with the One Ring, the most unnerving thing for the quartet of friends was to experience peace after returning to the Shire. An emergency room surgeon who works with people who have experienced trauma told me how, when he gets off a long shift of dealing with victims of car accidents, stabbings, and shootings, he'll leave the hospital "expecting the world to be on fire." In other words, it was unsettling to him to walk out of the ER and see that everything outside was fine. He viewed it all as a façade; it was almost as though the peace he saw was fake.

I felt exactly the same way when I returned from Afghanistan. I expected the world to be on fire, dark and gloomy, not what it really was. When I was in combat, I had to be so worried, getting up at the slightest sound. We had to drive in the tire tracks of the armored vehicle in front of us in case there was an explosive device buried right next to the ruts in the road. Veterans return home and find themselves driving in tire tracks here or wanting to have a buddy with them everywhere they go, because they are calibrated to live with a level of violence that isn't present in a peaceful location. The same is true for people who have gone through abusive childhoods. They become so used to walking on eggshells that when they are in a household that doesn't have any violence, they become weirded out by it, needlessly unsettled in a situation where it is peaceful.

In *The Return of the King*, Tolkien dedicates an entire chapter, "The Scouring of the Shire," to when the hobbits came back and how unnerved they were that they no longer had to travel in groups or be armed. They were shocked by it, and they didn't know how to reintegrate at first. While some of the hobbits eventually readjusted to their new normal, Frodo found that he was unable to do so. He isolated himself and slipped into growing depression, including increased anxiety on the anniversary of the day he was stabbed by the leader of the Nazgul. Aragorn commented that if Frodo allowed the wound to fester, he'd become like the Nazgul: not dead but also not alive. One day, when his best friend Sam came by his hobbit-hole to cheer him up, Frodo lamented, "I have been too deeply hurt, Sam. I tried to save the Shire, and it has been saved, but not for me. It must often be so, Sam, when things are in danger: some one has to give them up, lose them, so that others may keep them."

Not long after this, Frodo chose to leave the Shire and live with the elves. In the popular theatrical release of the trilogy, produced by Peter Jackson, this is seen as a joyful time, but I don't believe Tolkien originally meant it that way. What it signified was Frodo's inability to ever heal from the trauma he had endured. He never found a way to readjust to life in the Shire like the others had, so he had to leave. He lost his home. He lost his friends. He lost everybody. This can easily be seen as a metaphor not for healing, but for suicide.

That is the unintended, harsh reality so many military veterans are coming home to today. They fought bravely and made it home alive, yet they never really "come home." Some of my military friends, the ones who are able to readjust, actually lose contact with the ones who don't, and they feel that separation. If they can't learn to reconnect with their world again, they won't be able to heal and move beyond what happened to them—nurturing the horrible roots of what we now know as Post-Traumatic Stress Disorder (PTSD).

While we will cover PTSD in *Fellowship of Suffering*, it is not a term I like using very much because it carries with it a lot of assumptions. When people hear PTSD, they immediately think of combat veterans—but not everyone who has PTSD has been to war, and of all those who have been in combat, not all of them deal with what they have been through in the same ways.

What we will explore in *Fellowship of Suffering* is trauma and how it is processed. Even though the types of trauma we each experience are vastly different, our coping mechanisms and symptoms are surprisingly similar. One of the unfortunate things about labels like PTSD is that they tend to make people believe they will never be able to relate to or understand those who are enduring trauma. But when we see the similarities in our struggles, we can build bonds with one another through our suffering that allow for increased unity and fellowship to help us process and heal from most of our trauma while learning to cope with the wounds that will never fully be healed. The establishment of these bonds can then create within us something that we might have once thought was impossible: Post-Traumatic Growth, the process that brings about real and positive emotional and psychological development directly from our past trauma.

Fellowship of Suffering will explain what PTSD is and where it comes from, and it will reveal both my own experience with trauma and the negative coping mechanisms that we can adopt to try to cover over our pain. My desire is to share the wonderful hope we can have for healing and growth in God. My goal is to help anyone who has experienced trauma realize that you are not alone and that there is hope to alleviate your suffering. I also want to encourage those of you who are trying to help someone through their trauma to better relate to them and to equip you to use suffering as a means to draw closer to each other instead of allowing trauma to isolate you from one another.

When I began writing this book in 2019, I had healed enough so that my parents and I could begin going deeper with each other for the first time. Though I knew of their past, we truly discussed traumas they had experienced. My father was abandoned by his dad as a kid and his mom was an alcoholic. His stepfather was horribly abusive. My mother was abandoned in Korea and was an orphan. She was adopted into a family where she experienced abuse.

I never really knew—never really understood—how that stuff impacted them, until we were able to get together and embrace each other's suffering. That fostered understanding, a bond, and healing. It was restorative and life changing.

The same thing can happen for you.

Chapter 1
Coping to Become Numb

Because of the ongoing war on terror, the reality of PTSD has become a constant in our society. We are seeing more and more that even military veterans who return home physically unscathed are damaged in much deeper ways. This has caused us to begin evaluating the impact that trauma has on everyone, not just veterans. The first thing to understand about PTSD is that it isn't just something that happens to a certain group of individuals, but to anyone exposed to severe trauma, whether it be from combat, witnessing a death or violent event, being attacked or abused physically or emotionally, or some other type of disturbing or harmful event.

Secondly, PTSD is a sort of mental scar that is left on us after a traumatic experience. Normally, when you go through a distressing or disturbing event, your mind naturally processes it and creates a memory that you can access. When you make a memory, even if it is a particularly negative one, you can always look back on it in safety knowing that the experience is in the past and can't hurt you. However, when something really traumatic happens to you, your mind refuses to process the event correctly. Instead, it frantically attempts to suppress and ignore what happened in order to shield you from pain. When this occurs, your subconscious mind will then try to process it anyway. This sometimes happens in your dreams, usually through vivid nightmares, but it can also leave you susceptible to "triggers" that make you relive your trauma and overreact to situations in the present moment. Your exaggerated response comes because you aren't actually reacting to what is really happening, but to the unresolved trauma of your past.

When I came home from my first deployment, I remember going to a celebration with my friend, Chris, in his hometown of Saltville, Virginia. We served in different line companies in the same combat theater, and we were together in Saltville to see some fireworks. As the pyrotechnics exploded over our heads, even though we were ready for the sound, we immediately hit the deck! It was just like we were under fire back in Afghanistan. But it wasn't a response to the fireworks. We were reacting to the trauma of being shot at a few months prior to that on the battlefield.

That simple example illustrates what it means to be triggered. Something happens in the present that reminds you of your past experience and prompts you to relive a piece of your trauma. It will feel just as fresh as the day it actually happened. You aren't remembering your past. You are experiencing it all over again.

Let's say you were physically or emotionally abused as a child. Whenever someone raises their voice at you, you are transported back to being a helpless little boy or girl, causing you to freeze up and lose the ability to communicate. Maybe you built up so much rage as a child, it enabled you to fight back, so when someone confronts you with any amount of aggression, you disproportionately overreact. You blow up, becoming verbally or even physically harmful to the other person. It's not that you are fighting with them, but with your past abuser. In that moment, you may know you are responding more forcibly than is justified, but you won't admit it or be able to stop yourself if you do acknowledge it. The scary thing about these triggers is that they can be just about anything: a loud noise, someone yelling, seeing something that reminds you of your past, a particular smell, a specific person, or something completely random.

For most people, these triggers will only have an effect for a short amount of time. After a

13

few months or so, the symptoms will abate and go back to normal. This is Acute Stress Disorder (ASD) and is a short-term form of PTSD that almost everyone will experience at some point in their lives. However, there are some who won't get better, but progressively worse. For those people, their symptoms might be minor at first, but over time they become unbearable and uncontrollable. That is true PTSD. There are many reasons why people develop full-blown PTSD, such as the severity or length of their trauma, their mental state, or the kind of personal support system they may or may not have. Regardless of the reason, the way to determine if you have ASD or PTSD is to ask, "Over time, are my symptoms getting better or worse?"

As crippling and horrific as PTSD can be, the beautiful truth is there is hope to heal and cope with the symptoms. Some will fully heal; others won't. But they can learn how to carry on and function.

Developing coping mechanisms
When I look back, the first thing I recognize is the damage that occurred before I even went to Afghanistan. It's amazing to me how the infantry in the military tends to draw a particular personality type to its ranks. Those who gravitate toward the infantry have to be people who are willing to kill and who accept the real possibility that they will be killed at a young age.

For reasons still unknown to me, I grew up being a very angry person. I struggled to find my place in school, and never felt like I fit in or that anyone really understood me. I had friends, but none of my friendships were ever that close. It's likely that a childhood accident contributed to my difficulties. When I was 11, I was skiing with my family when I fell, slid down a steep incline, and hit my head on the base of a tree. I was not wearing any protective gear, and I slammed so hard I sprained my spine. My temple was scratched in three places, and I was taken to the hospital—but I was released the next day. I didn't receive a computed tomography (CT) scan or any other special treatment, but I did receive an x-ray.

After the accident, my parents told me they saw a noticeable shift in my personality. They said I went from being an energetic, lively, outgoing, creative, and personable kid to becoming a total recluse. I was not active. I stopped participating in sports. I stayed in the house. I didn't hang out much with my friends during the time I was becoming a teenager when I should have been learning to interact with my peers. According to my parents, it wasn't until I was about 16 that I began to revert to the way I was before.

Back then, no one knew much about traumatic brain injury (TBI), but I'm convinced, based on the symptoms I exhibited afterward, that I incurred a TBI that day on the slopes. Interesting, too, was how I felt two years later when I was told about my father's dad. I was a mess by then. I was totally rebelling against my parents and their faith, declaring myself to be an atheist. They told me about how my grandpa got blown up during World War II. What exactly happened to him in combat isn't clear, but the blast certainly did something to him. He eventually left his family and abandoned my dad. I never had any relationship at all with my grandpa, but I remember feeling some sort of a weird connection to him because I knew something was different with me. To this day, I don't how to explain it.

I also thought about things most kids didn't. I contemplated death, not just my own, but the reality that those around me were going to eventually die. My parents tell of me coming into their room almost every night, starting when I was about four, and standing at their bedside.

They'd ask me what was wrong, and I'd say, "I don't want to die." They didn't know what I was talking about. They tried to comfort me. "Well, Peter, when we die, we go to heaven." I always responded, "No, I don't want to live forever. If I did, I'd get bored because there are only so many things I could do for eternity." I argued with them out of a deep fear of dying, and of them dying, that consumed me.

I was mature enough then to understand that I didn't want to die, but not mature enough to be able to deal with those fears. They continued my entire life, and there was no trigger for this fear that I know of. The earliest I knew of a family member who died was when I was an early teenager. But since I felt that fear of death all the time, I found ways to shut out those emotions and convince myself that they didn't bother me. I learned to ignore them, suppress them, and not think about them. But as I numbed myself to my fear, it began to make me feel meaningless and ultimately insignificant. Therefore, when I got to the age where I could join the military, the concept of dying didn't bother me. The concept of killing didn't, either. In addition, the military attracted me because I wanted to have a life that mattered, and in the end, a death that mattered. I wanted to belong, and I needed a place to channel my anger and frustration.

Surprisingly, when I began my military service, I found that I could relate to most of those who were with me. It's not that everyone thought the exact same way I did, but I found a camaraderie from the fact that most of us felt a great deal of rage and annoyance toward the world. We also made sarcastic jokes about our pain and suffering and didn't value things, including our own lives, the way most other people did. Underneath it all was buried an insecurity we tried to block out that longed for recognition, significance, and respect. We wanted people to look up to us.

While the military didn't create these traits in us, our training was purposefully designed to increase these personality defects. Why? The United States military, and virtually every other military around the world, must produce soldiers who are willing to kill. Soldiers who care too much about themselves, much less others, won't do too well in combat. They'd constantly worry about what was happening with their families back home, and they certainly wouldn't be able to keep on fighting after watching their friends die. When one of my friends got shot or blown up, or even when I was shot and later blown up, unless I was physically unable to go on, I couldn't just take a day off to recover. I went right back out on patrol, sometimes within hours of the trauma.

In order to train us, we were taken on field ops that constantly tested us and made us miserable in every way. We went out in the worst weather imaginable without the provisions we needed. There were times in the rain without tents, the snow without jackets, and any condition without enough food, water, or rest. At first, we believed this was being done out of incompetence. We thought our leaders were idiots. Then, during my first deployment, one of my fellow Marines received two books called *On Combat* and *On Killing*. They were written by Dave Grossman, a lieutenant colonel who studied the psychology of combat and killing. He discussed how the training we were receiving was actually intentional. He wrote, "You know that someone is ready for combat and killing when they respond to trauma with laughter." The first time that happened to me on a field op was when we were left out in the snow minus our jackets, and instead of becoming sad we decided to do a silly dance contest. Something meant to be traumatic made us happy.

Of course, that happiness wasn't genuine, but just a coping mechanism. Over time, our leaders incessantly gave us false hope, promising vacations that never happened and a better life that never came. Eventually, this inflamed our apathy. We simply stopped caring and became more cold, bitter, and cynical, void of all hope. In the end, the goal was achieved. We became soldiers who were willing to die and who wouldn't be bothered or shaken by the realities of combat.

Essentially, this training pushed us toward becoming sociopaths—and if you are trained well enough, your odds of having PTSD actually go down. You can't traumatize someone who is already emotionally dead.

Comfortably numb

It is very common for people to attempt to suppress their emotions and convince themselves they aren't bothered by pain, sadness, regret, or trauma. While this can seem like a good way to cope because it can make you seem emotionally resilient and even tough, there are severe side effects to this approach. How can you truly love and have compassion on others when you have been conditioned to not care or show weakness? How can you possibly empathize with someone else's emotions when you spend all your time running from your own?

It's still very hard for me to identify and sympathize with those around me. When I hear other people's problems, my knee jerk reaction is to make a joke out of it or tell them to get over it and grow up. My way of coping with any negative emotion or problem was to jest and not care at all. I didn't realize that piece by piece, I was destroying my ability to love or have passion about anything. The level to which you are able to suppress your emotions is the degree by which you will struggle with compassion and empathy toward others.

How cold had I become? Before military personnel deploy, they are given a couple weeks of leave to spend time with loved ones. When my leave was up, I was about to get on the plane that was going to take me away from my home and parents and one step closer to combat in Afghanistan. My mom was weeping because her youngest son, a kid who was only 19 years old, was about to leave and possibly never come back. Yet I remember looking at her and my dad as I walked toward the security entrance of the airport and feeling absolutely *nothing*. No fear. No sadness. Just curiosity about why they were so sad. That apathy and ability to compartmentalize my emotions protected me from experiencing severe PTSD, but at what cost? Sometimes, I think the cure was worse than the disease.

The military trained me to be cold and empty so I could experience the hell of combat and be willing to lay down my life without a second thought. But what happens when someone who had resigned themselves to die comes back alive? Many in that situation don't see it as a problem. Their coping capacity became so strong and effective they often see it as a strength. I was that way, and it took me years to see the flaw in that reasoning as I realized my ability to experience passion, joy, hope, or love was missing. I was crushed. I didn't want to shut out all of those good things. But I was slowly and surely becoming more numb—comfortably numb—and I realized I couldn't pick and choose. I couldn't suppress negative emotions and at the same time delight in positive emotions. It really was all or nothing, and I was hopeless because I had no idea how to fix what had been broken. I believed I was doomed to be numb for the rest of my life.

Not everyone, of course, was as shut off as I was. No matter how hard they try or how rigorously they are trained, some people simply can't deaden their emotions. For them, the coping mechanism of suppressing their emotions and convincing themselves they aren't bothered by anything is more like putting a heavy lid on a pot of boiling water. It's effective for a time, but eventually the pot will boil over. When the regret, shame, sorrow, and fear start to return and are more violent and powerful than ever, it's easy to self-medicate with alcohol or other substances just to keep their emotions at bay. But this only works for a short period of time. They wear off and the effects of the trauma reemerge.

Unfortunately, simply telling yourself things don't bother you doesn't make it true. Repressing memories doesn't make them go away. Eventually, the waves of negative emotion hit you again and again as you are triggered in your daily life until you are controlled by them. This can cause you to become completely dependent on substances for any relief from your pain.

Trying to remain comfortably numb from your trauma can have an even worse effect on you because you might accidentally cut off the source of your emotion. If you recognize you are being triggered by past events, you may struggle as you wrestle through your extreme emotions, but you are far better off than someone who consistently represses and inadvertently cuts off their anchor to their emotions. Why? Not only can it become impossible for you to identify triggers, but your emotional state can't be worked on because there is nothing to address. Your emotions are no longer responsive. They're just the way they are.

I became so adept at repressing my feelings that when I got back from my first deployment, I was told by a therapist that I had a dissociative disorder. Dissociative disorders are mental disorders that involve experiencing a disconnection and lack of continuity between thoughts, memories, surroundings, actions, and identity. People with dissociative disorders escape reality in ways that are involuntary and unhealthy and cause problems with functioning in everyday life. Symptoms—ranging from amnesia to alternate identities—depend, in part, on the type of dissociative disorder. There are three types: dissociative amnesia, dissociative identity disorder, and depersonalization-derealization disorder. I had the latter. Technically, I still do.

If personality is viewed on a spectrum, with one side being healthy and the other side being a sociopath, I lean toward the sociopath side. Sociopaths are able to completely disassociate any emotions of guilt, or anything like that, so they can kill, rape, or abuse, and they won't feel anything. That leaning enabled me to avoid full-on PTSD, but it also created a tendency that I had to address through therapy after my return. I couldn't remember why I was so angry or cynical. That didn't stop me, though, from constantly feeling that way. I was "successful" in my coping methods, but none of what I did healed me. It only made me worse.

Among other things with depersonalization-derealization disorder, whenever I make a new memory, the disorder causes me to naturally smother and repress any emotions related to that memory. That causes me to compartmentalize pain and forget trauma rather easily. Unfortunately, it also takes away my ability to retain memories, good or bad. I don't know if my depersonalization-derealization disorder will ever truly go away. It's weird, because it is easy for most people to make and hang onto memories. They don't have to think about it. But I have to actively try to remember and solidify things in my mind. It is like there is something broken in me that comes naturally for everybody else. Sometimes, it's as if I have forgotten how to breathe, and I have to mentally tell myself, "inhale, exhale." I am improving, though, thanks in large part to spiritual realizations and disciplines I'll share in Chapter 3.

Dr. Courtney Warren, an expert on psychotherapy, eating disorders, addictions, and self-deception, says most people lie to themselves to ignore their real issues and problems. During a TED Talk, she said about past trauma, "As adults, we will most want to lie about how psychologically painful realities experienced as children affected who we are today ... As an adult, when someone points out your imperfections, you feel tremendous anxiety but deny where it comes from. Perhaps you felt ugly as a child because you were teased for your appearance. You learned to eat in response to emotional pain. As an adult, you struggle to maintain a stable weight, because your eating has very little to do with hunger. Perhaps you watched your parents fight. You learned to avoid conflict. Now, you struggle to admit even feeling negative emotion. Although each of our specific childhood learnings will be unique, what we learned will be exemplified in the lies we tell ourselves as adults."[i]

The most unfortunate thing about this type of self-deception is that even though we think we are helping ourselves by ignoring our pain, the hurt never really goes away. Instead, it manifests itself in the way we treat other people, react to our emotions, and adopt addictions and bad habits to help distract us from the truth of our pain. If we can't be honest about our pain, we lose our ability to heal from our past and to change in the future.

He feeds on ashes; A deceived heart has turned him aside; And he cannot deliver his soul, Nor say, "Is there not a lie in my right hand?"
Isaiah 44:20, NKJV

Chapter 2
Anger, Guilt, and Isolation

When we're unable to turn off our emotions, we can turn to three responses in an attempt to snuff out our pain, regret, and anxiety.

The first is *anger*, an especially attractive option for many people dealing with PTSD. The reason most of us are trapped in the trauma of the past is the sense that we could've, or should've, done more to prevent what happened. We can feel like helpless bystanders as we experience our past and are incapacitated by the paralyzing fear that kept us from doing "all we could" to stop it. We can endure the crushing regret and shame that comes from making a horrible decision that ended up severely damaging or killing someone else. This can frustrate us and cause us to turn to anger as we tell ourselves, "I will never be helpless again," or try to convince ourselves, "It wasn't my fault."

Sometimes we can convince ourselves that what is happening right now warrants a severe reaction. I got out of the military after two deployments, both in combat. My experiences during those deployments made me a cynical, sarcastic person who felt angry and apathetic. A year after getting out of the military, my friends and I were on a trip in California to make a film about prostitution for the nonprofit organization, Running Light. Our goal was to interview men and women who had been victims of human trafficking. I was driving, and the filmmaker, Caleb, was in the back of the car with an assistant, Anissa. A photographer and interviewer, Katie, was sitting in the passenger seat up front.

We were using his GPS, and it was telling us to cut through Camp Pendleton, near Oceanside, as a faster route to get to our destination in San Diego. I was well familiar with Pendleton. I'd spent one month there as part of my boot camp training and then did another three months at the camp when I did my SOI (School of Infantry) training—both prior to my first deployment to Afghanistan. Just being on the base had upped my anxiety.

As we started driving through Pendleton as directed by Caleb's GPS, I told everyone we shouldn't follow it. Military bases are equipped with chameleons, devices that disrupt radio signals. This is done, for example, so that the signal to electronics such as IEDs (improvised explosive devices) won't work. On top of that, his GPS was telling us to drive straight through a shooting range. I knew this was an open range where infantry go to train with weapons, artillery, and explosives. Just thinking about all that definitely put me on a razor's edge.

The GPS directed us toward a dirt road, and I repeated my earlier warning, my voice louder than before. "We cannot go down there."

"But the GPS is telling me," he responded from behind. He was quite calm and matter of fact about the whole thing, and that bothered me.

I started screaming at the top of my lungs. "I *told* you we can't go down here! This is a dead end. We are gonna get shot!" I braked the car, turned it around, and headed the other way. I wanted to throw his phone with the GPS out the window.

I totally shut him down. Everyone sat in stunned silence.

My heart was thumping and every nerve in my body was tingling. I used my previous knowledge of Pendleton's layout to get us back to one of the two main roads to start heading off the base. I tried to settle myself down. It stayed dead quiet for about 20 minutes.

Still on base, we eventually pulled over to a gas station. Caleb and Anissa went inside, and Katie came up next to me as I was putting fuel in the car. A nurturing person, she leaned toward me. "Peter, you need to apologize to him."

"Why do I need to apologize to him?" I replied, adrenaline surging again. "He almost got us killed!"

Katie remained quiet and steady. "What you just did to him reminded him of being a kid. He grew up with a verbally abusive dad."

When we were all back in the car and ready to pull out, I turned and looked at Caleb. "Sorry."

It wasn't really an actual apology. *He's a guy,* I thought. *He can get over it.*

During the incident, I actually did see the cause of my anger. I stopped us before we were in any real danger. I could've simply said, "Hey man, that's the shooting range. We shouldn't go down there." I could have done it very calmly, but I overreacted. When it was over, I knew I had been kind of a jerk, but I didn't want to admit it.

Everyone in the car was negatively affected that day. I didn't know it at the time, but one of the other passengers came from a verbally abusive background as well.

Caleb said he forgave me, and we had another two hours or so to get to San Diego. Once we got there, things went back to normal. But it was clear I had hurt all those around me with my anger.

Military veterans can have such extreme anger problems, not just because we were trained in our aggression, but because anger becomes another coping mechanism. We get worse as our anger burns like fire and requires more fuel to stay ablaze. That anger, with its constant violent overreactions, can end up pushing away everyone around us through the bitter behavior that comes along with it.

As unresolved anger seethes within us, we create new reasons to be unhappy and stir up strife as we sulk in our past and ruminate about how upset we are with the people we believe are responsible for what happened to us. We also ignite arguments within our relationships and become increasingly self-destructive, all in a subconscious attempt to quiet our negative emotions with our wrath. This prevents us from admitting when we are wrong because we have to justify our anger. No wonder Proverbs 15:18 rightly declares, "A wrathful man stirs up strife, but he who is slow to anger allays contention." (NKJV)

We will never deal with the brokenness within us by ignoring it through rage. Even though our anger can be a distraction from our pain, if we never process our past, we will always be susceptible to the effects of PTSD. It is emotion that anchors us to our past. Our most vivid past experiences, both positive and negative, are tied to powerful emotional experiences. Therefore, when we turn to anger to overcome our issues, it actually serves to anchor us deeper and deeper into our past, making our traumas more powerful over time. We do this by ruminating. Let's say you get into an argument with your spouse and leave the room. You may ruminate about it by sitting and rolling the disagreement over and over in your mind. "I could have said this," or "I really should have done that," or "I wish I had told her off." Truth is, the argument may have been mundane, not that big of a deal, and maybe it ended very quickly. But because you are ruminating about it, you are actually making it worse than it really was.

The same is true of your past. Perhaps you dated someone for a long time, but it ended in a breakup. The emotion you should be feeling is loss. You miss that person. Instead, you go back in your memory and start changing what really happened in the relationship. You should be feeling sad, but instead you're becoming angrier. Someone will talk to you about it, and you'll say, "I didn't realize what a manipulative, horrible, deceptive, vindictive person I was dating until now." What you've done is taken even happy memories and altered them. In the process, you are also making them that much more vivid. Your trauma is made more powerful over time, but it is really much more than that. You are rewriting history and solidifying that revised memory in your mind. It is easier to recall, but it isn't necessarily what happened. It is your version of the relationship. We can do the same thing with positive memories, adding a few things here and there, to create a heightened sense of nostalgia.

All of us do this to a certain extent, but when people who have traumatic pasts ruminate in this way, they are also trying to rewrite their feelings of regret, loss, and helplessness. They feel they should've done more to address the trauma. In a weird way, they are trying to forget because they don't want to feel that way anymore, when all they are actually doing is making the event easier to remember. I've talked to combat vets from Vietnam who are in their seventies. Their memories aren't what they used to be, but they can tell you about their time in Vietnam like it was yesterday. It is still locked in.

Potentially more destructive than anger toward others is when we turn our anger *inward*. When we do this, we may begin to hate ourselves for being so helpless and weak. We can also bury ourselves in regret over the wrong things we believe we have done. As guilt and shame eat away at us from the inside, we'll push others away because we feel unworthy. If, for example, you sit down with a father who abandoned his kids and his family and became an alcoholic, he'll say, "I'm no good for them." In other words, he wanted to be rejected because he felt so unworthy of their care or affection. He felt he was getting what he deserved. In these situations, people can easily become self-destructive and have no regard for their own safety.

Attempting to silence the guilt

In addition to becoming soldiers who were willing to die and who wouldn't be troubled by the realities of combat, we also had to be willing to kill. In most places, it's considered wrong to even talk about killing people, much less be taught how to do so, but in the infantry, killing was part of our daily conversation. We were always training, shooting at targets that looked like people, grappling with our fellow Marines to practice and perfect new fighting techniques, and learning combat strategies. As we took in all this intense, stress-producing training, it made us more aggressive and bitter—and that, in turn, made it more acceptable for us to think about killing others.

So why don't combat veterans turn into serial killers? Our military leaders told us that killing people was wrong, but they also subtly taught us that the enemy wasn't human. This is why most veterans will use racial slurs or the name of the military to refer to the people they fought. World War II vets will talk about fighting Krauts, or Japs, or Nazis, while veterans from the current war will say they fought Hadjis, ISIS, Al Qaeda, or the Taliban. This allows them to slowly convince themselves that they aren't actually killing people, just "the enemy." The reason for doing this is obvious: it is the most effective way to get soldiers to kill their enemy without remorse, but at the same time does not turn them into killers outside of their military duty.

Problem is, when we're overseas in the combat theater, everyone thinks the same, but when we come home and tell our friends and family our war stories, they look at us with shock or terror. That begins to tear down our belief that we weren't actually killing other human beings. That's one of the reasons why PTSD has seemingly gotten worse in recent years, even though the wars in Iraq and Afghanistan, as horrible as they are, are way less bloody than previous conflicts. It's not that previous veterans didn't struggle with PTSD, but back in World War II, the country was filled with patriotism. Everyone believed that the war our troops were fighting was a righteous endeavor and treated all our veterans like heroes. Americans, in general, truly believed the U.S. military hadn't been killing "people," but the Axis Powers, so they supported the veterans in all of their actions. Around the time of Vietnam, however, public opinion changed as the war became something Americans could watch on the news. They *saw* footage of the carnage and death, and this caused people to turn on our troops and accuse them of being murderers and child killers.

When someone who has killed others in the line of duty hears that, it causes them to only see the dark side of their nature, and they will start to think of themselves as a monster. The subsequent guilt can permanently damage their psyche and cause them to mentally break down to the point where they can't recover. They may even begin to act more like a monster because that is what they believe they are. While public opinion is far more positive today than it was in the Vietnam era, veterans still can't escape the fact that they were involved in the killing of actual people—and this can cause them to see themselves as nothing more than a murderer.

Because of my personality disorder, this never really happened to me like it did to most of my friends from my two deployments. They were swayed by what other people thought because they saw themselves as being in community with others. Therefore, if one of my fellow Marines talked to someone at home about being in a firefight in combat and the person responded with shock, my friends became angry and defensive as a way to deal with their guilt. On the other hand, I dismissed people outright. Instead of thinking, "Oh my gosh, they're right. I am a monster," I just thought, "They're wrong, and I don't care." But that pushed me away, causing me to feel alienated from my friends and family. It fed my narcissism and made me feel that much more alone.

One of the guys with whom I deployed was a sergeant from the south who had already been on five other deployments. He'd been shot four times, once in the brachial artery. It was incredible he was still alive. But he kept going back. Once, during the war in Iraq, he told an interviewer about his deployment, "I love it. It's like a hunting trip. I get to go out and defend my country and put down the dogs that are coming to get us." He didn't see anything wrong with what he was doing. It was his way of handling his guilt. He's the same kind of guy who could come home and play Call of Duty for hours on end, racking up the kills in an online competition with other players and enjoying every moment. It's cathartic, but also a way to continue managing guilt.

Yet it's hard to turn off that killing mentality. There's a simplicity to being in combat. Someone does something wrong and you kill them. Then you come home, see an injustice, and think, "We should just kill those people." Or they'd see people of Middle Eastern descent in the grocery store and have to actively avoid them for fear of having a flashback and wanting to harm them, right there in the produce aisle. All are responses intended to assuage their guilt.

Drowning in isolation

The number one thing that can cause someone's life to spiral out of control is isolation. Human beings can undergo severe amounts of pain and trauma, and as long as they have a community where they feel loved and understood, they can cope. But when someone feels alone and cut off, hopelessness sets in and traumatic wounds fester and grow.

I never saw anyone get PTSD while we were in Afghanistan. It was only when we came home that it started. Why? When we were in a community where our trauma was shared and, to whatever extent, understood, we weren't traumatized because it was our norm. But when we got home and started seeing our lives through the eyes of those who hadn't shared our experiences, we began to realize that what we had done and what we had gone through was not normal at all. We recognized the dysfunction of combat, and the shame and trauma from our actions caused us to feel like we were alone. The same dynamic is true for anyone. When you share your trauma with another person and they try to love you by listening to your pain, they may accidentally make your issues worse by reacting negatively to what you are sharing with them.

When my friends and family reacted with shock and disbelief to my combat experiences, it made me feel more isolated than ever. They didn't mean to hurt me, but what I was describing was so foreign to them, they didn't know what else to do. But that prompted me to start listening to my fears that I was now so different, there was no way I could relate to them any longer. That caused me to not want to share anything, and that increased my shame about what I had done. When others, like Caleb and my friends, reacted negatively to my violent outbursts, or even tried to excuse my behavior by saying, "Oh, you've been to war. It's okay," it was like a knife in my chest. I felt more and more alien to those I loved. Deep down, I felt judged and misunderstood, and in my isolation, my brokenness grew. I didn't have the strength of a community who understood me.

Community, and the atmosphere it creates, is vital to well-being. In 1978, Canadian psychologist Bruce K. Alexander wanted to challenge the belief that it was the substances alone that caused addiction. Researchers worldwide had done countless experiments where they locked rats in cages and hooked them up to intravenous tubes that dispensed narcotics to the animals if they pushed a lever. In every case, the rats ignored their natural instincts and became hopeless addicts or overdosed and died.

The problem Alexander saw with this research was that these rats, who are social creatures, were trapped alone in a cage with nothing to do but get high. So, he and his team revamped the experiment with what he called a "rat park," a whole community of rats with two sources of water: one laced with narcotics and the other that was pure. He found that the rats drank from the water that was laced a few times, but then decided as a group to stick with pure water. He even took rats that were already addicted to narcotics and put them in the rat park to see if they would continue in their addiction.

To his surprise, every one of the previously addicted rats willingly went through withdrawals to become sober with the rest of the community in the rat park. Alexander proved that the source of addiction and self-destructive behavior was not primarily the substance itself, but the environment. Remove isolation and create community, and the group worked out the problem in a healthy way.

When they were in the military, combat vets felt understood, but when they left, they felt isolated because no one really understood them. That isolation made their existing trauma worse and more unbearable, resulting in PTSD. They lacked a new community where they felt accepted and where healing choices existed. They needed a "rat park."

As bad as our situation was in Afghanistan, I don't know anyone who struggled or committed suicide while we were over there. We could be ourselves, and we had hope that when we got home, everything would get better. Then we got home and realized we were like strangers in our homes and communities. Our problems and inner pain didn't get better, but worse. When those feelings of hopelessness begin to consume a person's psyche, and they are constantly triggered and consumed by negative emotions, suicide can seem like the only measure of control and relief available to them.

That's why some vets, like the sergeant from the south, keep going back. It's the only place where they feel they belong and are understood. But people who do this can find that they can only function in war. Peace terrifies them, and they bring that aggression back with them and pour it out on their families. Those who aren't veterans can do this over and over as well as they seek out chaos that is familiar to them. Children who are abused often end up in relationships where they are abused or abuse others. These dysfunctional environments and relationships might make us feel more normal, and while it can be argued that a dysfunctional relationship is better than no relationship at all, it will keep us from healthy, positive growth. We will continue to act out the dysfunction that is normal to us—unless we can find a new normal.

Anger, guilt, and isolation are harsh realities for the person who has endured trauma—but it doesn't have to be the end. It isn't easy and it isn't quick, but healing is possible. I have experienced more healing than I ever thought I could, and I know that there is more that needs to take place within me. I can confidently say that the greatest resources for help and healing are found in a relationship with God and the principles found in the Bible.

Oh, what a miserable person I am! Who will free me from this life that is dominated by sin and death? Thank God! The answer is in Jesus Christ our Lord.
Romans 7:24-25, NLT

Chapter 3
Treating the Spiritual and the Physical

It is important to recognize that modern psychology has progressed in leaps and bounds in its efforts to help those who struggle with a myriad of psychological disorders caused by both nature and nurture. No one should discount the potential positive impact of psychology because it has the power to genuinely help those who effectively employ it. For the Christian, these resources can bring great benefit in the same way physical medicine, when properly used, can foster health and well-being.

However, psychology alone falls short in that it does not take into account the importance of the human soul. The basis of modern psychology is almost exclusively materialistic, meaning that it must reduce everything down to psychological disorders and past trauma because the soul is not considered. But, for those who take seriously the claims of the Bible, the soul is a very real thing, and it is just as important as the mind to someone's mental health. In addition, if it is true that the prosperity of the soul can only be found in a genuine relationship with God, true peace or wholeness is not possible without addressing the most fundamental trauma of their existence: separation from God.

Jesus Christ came not only to die in our place that we might have forgiveness for our sins, but He also died so we could have union with our heavenly Father, for it is from this union that we can have true and genuine healing.

Unfortunately, there is a tendency within Christianity to think that when someone gets saved by accepting Jesus as their Lord and Savior, all of their problems magically go away. As Christians, we can also overemphasize our spiritual experience and believe that our bodies and minds are not that important to our overall well-being in comparison. It is for this reason that some Christians reject counseling and other forms of therapy outright because they don't feel its beneficial or necessary.

This is an example of "dualism," which states that the spiritual and the physical are completely separate and they have no real impact on one another—but this belief is completely foreign to the Bible. In the scriptural account of the creation of humanity, God forms us from the dirt and then breathes into us, making us a living soul (Genesis 2:7). This means that the original creation portrays a marriage between the physical and the spiritual. The two cannot be separated. Even in the resurrection of Christ, He wasn't merely raised spiritually, but physically, and it is through that physical resurrection that humanity has hope for the restoration of the physical universe, including the resurrection of our own physical bodies. (1 Corinthians 15, 2 Corinthians 5, 2 Peter 3:10-13, and Revelation 21-22 explore these concepts in detail.)

It is imperative to understand that our healing isn't an either/or proposition (addressing our physical or our spiritual beings), but it is a both/and issue (requiring both the physical and the spiritual to be addressed). As we accept this truth, we are then positioned to seek healing first and foremost in our relationship with God, and then utilize the vast and relevant resources available to take care of our minds and bodies.

Psalm 42:3 (NIV) begins with the words, "My tears have been my food day and night…" It was written by a man undergoing severe depression to the point that he stopped taking care of his physical body. To be more specific, he was so grief stricken, he had stopped eating or sleeping. It is common for people who are healing from trauma and experiencing things like panic attacks, anxiety, and depression to neglect their bodily health. This isn't done intentionally, but in the midst of their severe emotional pain, they forget to properly eat, sleep, exercise, or communicate with others. They also tend to turn to unhealthy habits, such as overeating or substance abuse, that make them feel better momentarily, but end up hurting them in the end. They don't understand the profound negative impact it'll have on their spiritual and psychological health.

God made us with a body, spirit, and mind, so ignoring our bodily health will have a massive impact on our ability to heal. One of the first things we need to do in order to begin this healing process is to be diligent in taking care of our physical health. We can make a list to ensure we are feeding, resting, and moving our bodies, staying sober, and getting enough vitamins to address the damage in our minds and spirits. Having a healthy body alone doesn't mean we will heal from our traumas, but when we stop seeing to our physical health, it can add an unnecessary burden as we try to look after our deeper spiritual and psychological needs.

This self-care principle applies to our mental health as well. In Isaiah 9:6 (NIV), Jesus is called our "Wonderful Counselor." One of the things God wants to do in His relationship with us is to counsel us on how to deal with our hurts. We are also encouraged throughout the Bible to become a part of the community He has given us and find good human counselors who can help us talk through our issues, provide helpful resources, and encourage us in our ultimate healing through God. Counseling is only effective when someone is willing to be honest about their traumas, humbly listen to advice, and apply it to start dealing with their pain.

Some Christians struggle with seeking counsel because they think to do so somehow shows a lack of faith or undermines the power of the Word of God and the Holy Spirit to work in us individually. That simply isn't true. The Bible and the divine revelation that comes from the Holy Spirit is what draws us to God. Nothing else can do that. Yet God has also given us amazing resources that can help us practically deal with the physical and mental problems we face in this fallen world. It is as foolish to ignore them as it would be for a Christian having a heart attack to not call the paramedics.

God alone is the source of *every* earthly resource and benefit that we enjoy. Through our relationship with Him and the tools He has given, healing can happen, but it doesn't happen automatically or without effort. James 2:17 says, "So also faith by itself, if it does not have works, is dead." (ESV) Simply *believing* that God can bring healing is not enough to deal with your specific issues. Employ the amazing resources He's provided, trusting that He will be faithful to heal us and draw us closer to Him as we do.

Sufficient grace

It is true that God can choose to miraculously heal physical and mental issues immediately, and we should pray for this type of healing. But if God doesn't choose to heal us instantly and supernaturally, it is no less beautiful or miraculous to receive from Him the grace necessary to rely on God for our gradual healing.

In 2 Corinthians 12:8-10, the Apostle Paul wrote, "Concerning this thing I pleaded with the Lord three times that it might depart from me. And He said to me, 'My grace is sufficient for you, for My strength is made perfect in weakness.' Therefore most gladly I will rather boast in my infirmities, that the power of Christ may rest upon me. Therefore I take pleasure in infirmities, in reproaches, in needs, in persecutions, in distresses, for Christ's sake. For when I am weak, then I am strong." (NKJV) Paul reveals that he prayed for instantaneous healing from God but didn't receive it. Instead, God responded to Paul in gentleness and love and promised him the grace necessary to sustain him in his suffering.

This might sound like an unloving reply, but that's only if we miss the point of true healing. Remember, our greatest problem is not our trauma or disorders. They pale in comparison to our real issue: our broken relationship with God. Even when this relationship is restored, it will still take consistent time and effort to grow in our relationship with Him. Because of this, God often gives His people grace to sustain us in our suffering as opposed to grace to deliver us from our pain. He does this because His strength is "made perfect" in us in our weaknesses. Healing is an unhurried, ongoing process.

When God simply delivers us from a problem, as awesome as that is, it moves us to a place where we don't have to daily press in to Him or seek Him to deal with our traumas. But when He gives us the grace to enable us to endure our pain, that causes us to seek and rely on Him daily, which brings us closer to Him than before. Plus, if what the Bible says about the supreme beauty of God is true, that He is infinitely pleasurable, far greater than anything in creation, then this miracle of sustaining grace can actually be viewed as superior to the miracle of delivering grace. As we become more dependent on Him, our affection for Him grows.

The idea of sustaining grace being better than delivering grace may be frustrating for some, but I can tell you from my own personal experience that I am thankful God didn't immediately heal me. His slow process of healing has brought me greater intimacy with God than I would've ever experienced otherwise—and it was because of this gradual healing that God has enabled me to address the deeper roots of my issues. It's just as Paul says in Philippians 3:8, "Indeed, I count everything as loss because of the surpassing worth of knowing Christ Jesus my Lord." (ESV)

This patient process of sustaining grace got underway for me as I was just beginning to grow in my walk with the Lord. I was at a church youth conference, and one of the speakers told the story of a time he felt God was impressing on him to pray for whatever it took to draw closer to Him. Because he sensed the Lord was preparing him for some sort of trial, he was afraid, but he believed God was telling him, "I've got you. It's gonna be okay." The same day he prayed that prayer, he was in a horrible motorcycle accident that fractured his skull and nearly took his life. The speaker went on to describe his healing process and how it brought to life a ministry idea within him while helping him move forward in his relationship with God. He said that time of weakness was vital.

I went home, and I experienced one of the rare times when I heard God speak audibly to me. I prayed, "God, whatever it takes, draw me closer to you," and He replied aloud, "What could I take from you that would matter?"

I instantly realized that I didn't care about anything or anyone. Then God said, "You think you are strong because you don't care, but it has made you a dead man. Dead men can't serve me." It totally broke me as I saw my inner brokenness and callousness toward all my emotions.

As God humbled me with the sobering truth of my broken state, He led me to His Word to find hope for my healing. That's when I read Ezekiel 36:26 for the first time. It says, "I will give you a new heart and put a new spirit within you; I will take the heart of stone out of your flesh and give you a heart of flesh." (NKJV) I felt like God was speaking that promise directly to me. Only He could remove my heart that I had made hard through years of trying to numb myself and give me a heart that would *feel* once again.

While I remember being scared of letting go of all of my coping mechanisms and learning to be vulnerable enough to have a heart that was soft, I knew it was the only way that I could be able to love others and experience genuine joy and healing. It was the first time I truly had hope God could do that work in my life.

The following week ended up being a difficult one. Everything that could go wrong seemed *to* go wrong. But in the midst of it all, I felt like God was giving me a choice: I could either compartmentalize the pain and ignore it, or I could go through it and feel it for the first time. I didn't know what I wanted to do. Then the Lord led me to the account of Christ's crucifixion where Jesus was offered an anesthetic, wine vinegar on a sponge attached to the stalk of the hyssop plant, to alleviate the excruciating pain He was experiencing on the cross. At first, He refused it, but later, right before He died, He took it.

I thought it was weird for Jesus to refuse it before the suffering and then take it after He had suffered. Then God helped me discern that Jesus was not suffering for Himself, but for me—and that He had to feel the suffering in its totality.

That's when the Lord asked me if I was willing to suffer for Him. I said "yes," and it was like falling without a net. I wondered how I was ever going to endure the pain without anything to numb me.

But I made it. God gave me sustaining grace.

Hope is essential. Without it, we can give up and say, "This is just the way I will always be." Healing will seem impossible, and we'll see ourselves as permanently damaged and become apathetic. I know. I did it for years—but when I discovered and believed that God really could heal me, it filled me with hope and gave me the courage to pursue that healing in Him.

Fellowship of suffering

Years ago, a man named Sebastian Junger, an American journalist, author, and filmmaker who spent a lot of time documenting conflicts in war zones across the globe, wrote a book entitled, *Tribe: On Homecoming and Belonging*. In it, he argued that the rise in PTSD was not primarily a result of the violence of our current wars, but the rising state of isolation and division within our own country. In order to prove this, he went around the world spending time with different tribal cultures who were constantly engaged in warfare.

What he found was that in close-knit, tribal communities, depression and PTSD were remarkably lower than what he found in the United States. Some of the places he visited didn't even have a word for PTSD because it is so nonexistent. Israel, for example, is essentially a Westernized nation, but it retains a tribal mindset—and that nation has a PTSD rate of less than one percent among their active military and veterans. Israel, in general, possesses a strong sense of community. Whatever they do, they are in it together and for the common good.

When Junger looked at America, however, he saw a society that was extremely individualistic with very little community. We can spend our entire day with strangers. We can go outside and walk among strangers, drive around strangers, work with strangers, and even live around strangers. We don't really know anyone. Junger found even less dedication to the common good in the United States. Because of this, he said American society is actually taking *away* from the three basic things humans need in order to be content. "They need to feel competent at what they do; they need to feel authentic in their lives; and they need to feel connected to others. These values are considered 'intrinsic' to human happiness and far outweigh 'extrinsic' values such as beauty, money and status."

The negative effects of these disordered priorities are notably seen in the lives of those who are trying to find healing from past wounds. For most veterans, when we are in the military, those basic needs are being met. We feel competent in our jobs and very necessary to the overall success of our unit. We feel authentic because we have the ability to communicate to those around us openly and without any filters. Finally, we feel deeply connected to those around us because of the shared time and experiences we have with one another.

But then we come home to a country divided as Junger described, and we no longer feel like we are necessary, have a clear understanding of what we are doing, or that we can be authentic. We become disconnected from those around us, and that intolerable feeling cultivates the pain of our trauma and makes it seem as though we can never move on from it.

This lack of community impacts everyone, playing a huge role in the rise of depression, anxiety, drug abuse, struggles in sexual relationships, and suicide. It can even be argued that a lack of community and belonging have created more sociopathic tendencies among some people. When you belong to a community, you feel responsibilities toward others that help replace selfishness and aggression with more benevolent activities. But if you don't feel like you belong to a group, it's easy to feel like society exists only to meet your needs, making you less concerned about others. As Junger observed, "As affluence and urbanization rise in a society, rates of depression and suicide tend to go up rather than down."

In modern society, many believe that scientific enlightenment, increased education, and growth in personal prosperity answer the fundamental needs of human happiness. Even in the realm of healing, the solution to our brokenness is not found in counselors and medications alone. Nothing replaces the need for community and genuine fellowship with others. Trauma can't be healed unless it is properly processed in the context of community rather than isolation.

This is true in Christian churches as well. The vast majority of church culture has been profoundly impacted by the way the culture as a whole is moving. It is hard to be authentic or genuine in a church setting. We struggle to be vulnerable, open up, and share about our sin, failures, and pain. Sadly, the very community God intended to bring the most amount of care, understanding, and comfort has become a place where most people expect (or have already experienced) judgment and shame instead of healing. When the majority of Christians struggle with trauma, their first instinct is to isolate as opposed to seeking genuine comfort in fellowship.

This is especially unfortunate because biblical authors saw pain and suffering as a mechanism for *increased* unity and fellowship. When Paul wrote Philippians 3:10-11, he had suffered the loss of every material blessing that he had as he was confined in a Roman prison. But in that dark and desolate place, he joyously wrote about the "fellowship of his sufferings" because he understood that suffering was one of the most powerful ways to build intimacy with someone else. Militaries make soldiers go through boot camp not just to train them for battle, but to break them down so that their shared trauma builds an instant, tight bond with other people they've never met. Combat veterans have the increased shared trauma from battle that makes us even more intimate with one another.

Paul recognized that his Savior wasn't someone who sat in heaven uncaring and immune to suffering but was One who took on the fullness of human suffering, even to the point of death. What this allowed Paul to realize was that he didn't have to hide his pain from a God who didn't understand. Rather, the more suffering he endured, the more unified he became to his God. When he suffered, Paul pressed deeper toward Christ, and it was that intimacy that enabled Paul to acknowledge and process what he was going through. His intimacy with God then extended to others in the early church. Even in the isolation of prison, Paul did not stop reaching out to those he knew. He wrote some of his most powerful and moving letters to the churches while alone and incarcerated as he kept his love for them fresh in his mind through prayer. The early church was arguably one of the most unified communities that ever existed—and the reason for this wasn't primarily shared belief, but shared suffering.

The Christian church in modern Western civilization is arguably the most prosperous church that has ever existed. It has access to more of the best resources for Bible study, doctrinal knowledge, and worship than anyone has ever enjoyed. Through the internet, writings from the most famous and influential church leaders in history are easily available, as are countless sermons being preached all over the world. There are seemingly endless amounts of worship music sung by the most talented musicians alive today. Yet, in spite of all this prosperity and the amazing resources on hand, the modern Western church is largely disunified. It doesn't have the oneness or the intimate fellowship and wholeness of the early church, and its members today largely mirror the anxiety and depression levels experienced by the general population in Western nations.[ii]

I would even go a step further and assert that the Western Christian church is doing far worse in the areas of unity and emotional stability than most of the persecuted church communities that are alive and well in the world today. I have heard so many people tell others that are going through suffering, "Listen to more sermons. Listen to more worship music. Read this book." While this advice isn't bad in and of itself, the use of such resources is not the solution. Otherwise, today's church would be more unified and emotionally sound than any church era before it. As good as these things are, they do not replace our implicit need for intimacy.

The early church was heavily persecuted, they were a small, minority group, and most of its members were totally illiterate, yet they were incredibly intimate with one another. Read through the letters of the apostles and the book of Acts, and their closeness and affinity for each other is quite evident. Even secular counselors who don't apply biblical principles recognize that if someone can't learn to reintegrate with their community, even if the symptoms of their trauma abate, they will never fully heal. If we want to heal and gain the kind of unity as Christians that the early church had, we have to learn how to engage with one another *in* our suffering as opposed to covering over our pain and acting like it isn't there.

This is especially difficult to do in Western society because of how sanitized we have become toward the topics of suffering and death. It is true that in the early church, and in persecuted churches today around the world, suffering was and is far more brutal and prevalent than it is in Western culture. However, that does not mean suffering and death are nonexistent.

They are realities in all societies regardless of how prosperous they are. What is different is how hard we try to purge ourselves from the existence of suffering and death in order to stave off our deep dislike and fear of both. It's why we try to usher people off to hospice care when they are dying, rush to cover bodies in a car accident, and overlook or underplay the grieving process.

In ancient cultures, as well as in many others today around the world, suffering and death were not covered over like this. It's not like those cultures celebrated trauma or loss, but they also did not try so desperately to hide it. People saw the bodies of the dead, buried their own family members, and their grieving processes were public and lengthy. This kind of practice brought about an understanding and familiarity with suffering and death. They were not seen as strange and shameful like they can be in our Western culture. While suffering and death were tragic, they were also normal and recognized openly.

Today's Christian church has a responsibility to make the difficult effort to not shy away from the painful realities of suffering and death. We should not pretend as if there is no need to mourn and grieve, covering over the pains of our past. We must be willing to uncover our traumas to others and learn to comfort and help one another. Everyone suffers, and all of us will face death in our lives. The promise of heaven does not take away these sorrows, but it does give comfort and hope within our sorrows and grief (1 Thessalonians 4:13). Because we have a Savior who suffered such brutality as publicly as He did, yet still openly bore the scars of His trauma (John 20 and 21), we should be able to gain the boldness to share our own traumas with one another and take part together in the fellowship of suffering.

Our experiences with suffering do not have to be identical in order for us to do this. While our past pain and trauma will be unique, there will be some overlap in the causes, and more importantly, the symptoms of our pain. To build a community of understanding and healing, we must be willing to invite our friends and family into our healing process and equip them to help us cope with and process our pain and grief.

This is certainly not an easy thing to do, especially when you get hurt and want to isolate and ignore your pain. But it is essential to healing. It's in isolation where you can become convinced that you are damaged and different from those around you. Even though you are the one who has been hurt, others do not naturally know how to help you. That's why you need to summon your bravery and strength to learn how to explain your issues and your needs to those around you, inviting them into your healing process. I encourage you to challenge yourself to take this step of faith. For those of you who want to help a loved one through this process, accept that you don't have to understand the depths of what they've been through to help them. More than anything else, they want to feel that they are not damaged beyond repair. Their trauma hasn't made them an alien. They need to know that they are loved and can still have a relationship with you.

Beloved, do not think it strange concerning the fiery trial which is to try you, as though some strange thing happened to you; but rejoice to the extent that you partake of Christ's sufferings, that when His glory is revealed, you may also be glad with exceeding joy.
1 Peter 4:12-13, NKJV

One reason Paul experienced the intimacy with Christ needed for him to acknowledge and process his suffering is because only God really understood how broken he was and what he needed in order to heal—and the same is true for us.

We are all broken in unique ways, so our responses to the traumas that break us will also be distinct. Some people come through it relatively okay. Others are more like me and develop strong coping mechanisms that make them dead emotionally. Many can be crippled psychologically and spiritually by guilt and anxiety. Therefore, healing varies for different people. For some, God will choose to give them a sudden and powerful deliverance from their issues, while others will experience a gradual healing that takes place over time. Many will never be fully healed, but instead receive the grace to lean on God in their brokenness and learn to cope with their symptoms.

Since we label people with disorders, we lump them into categories that can cause us to have preconceived notions about their diagnoses, symptoms, and traumas that then take away from their individual struggles and render us less effective, or totally ineffective, at understanding or helping them. This can cause those of us who don't have disorders to feel we can't possibly help or relate to people who do, or it might even make us afraid to aid those with disorders such as PTSD because they may think that all people with PTSD are violent. Even those who do assist people with PTSD might make the mistake of thinking that everyone's symptoms and healing process will be the same.

None of this is true, and these misconceptions can be very harmful. In *Tribe: On Homecoming and Belonging*, Junger observed that PTSD "is a disorder of recovery, and if treatment only focuses on identifying symptoms, it pathologizes and alienates vets. But if the focus is on family and community, it puts them in a situation of collective healing."

When we are helping people with trauma, before we can see their brokenness, we have to learn to see the individual. This is not easy to do, but if we identify someone only by their brokenness, we will actually make that person feel more ashamed and uncomfortable. As an associate pastor of a church, I attend a lot of funerals and make many hospital visits. In environments like that, we realize most of us just don't know what to say or how to act with someone who is hurting. We feel awkward and don't know if we should talk about things frankly and directly, act like nothing is wrong, or give that person space.

What I have learned is that when people are hurting, they don't need us to ask them how they are doing, press them about what they are going through, or bombard them with advice. They also don't need to be given too much space because that could make them feel they are a burden on everyone. Instead, we need to approach them as individuals, not as a broken thing that needs to be fixed. We can simply come as a friend, reaching out to them and seeking to spend time with them. As we do this over time, their brokenness will naturally come up as they see us as a safe place where they can be open and vulnerable.

Remember, we are all broken in the eyes of God. No one is perfectly whole. Jesus said it isn't those who are well who need a physician, but those who are sick (Matthew 9:12). It's not that the "well" are beyond the touch of His salvation. His point was that everyone is broken, and those who realize that and seek Him as their great physician will be blessed. The more we understand that as a community of believers in God, the more we will be able to admit to our own brokenness, which will free us from the stigma trauma creates. The more we appreciate the genuine commonality and fellowship of our shared brokenness, the more we will be able to build unity and foster healing with each other through our suffering.

Still, no matter how good we get at comforting one another, we can't fully understand each other's brokenness and individual needs. Proverbs 14:10 tells us, "The heart knows its own bitterness, And a stranger does not share its joy." (NKJV) Even more disturbing is that we can't fully understand our *own* needs and brokenness, but we can have peace knowing that Jesus does. As Proverbs 20:24 says, "A person's steps are directed by the Lord. How then can anyone understand their own way?" (NIV) Our healing must begin with intimacy with Christ, for He is the only One who really understands what we are going through, what we need, and can enable our healing to grow and develop in unity with others.

When we allow people to lump us and our brokenness into neat little categories, it can take away our individuality and create additional trauma that wasn't there before. Brokenness is a spectrum, and since we are not all broken in the same ways, we require personal attention. We need to trust God and seek His wisdom to reveal our individual sources of hurt and healing in Him. No matter what you've experienced and regardless of your past, God loves you and wants to meet you where you are. Having God with you and knowing that He alone fully understands you and cares for you is the first step forward in being made whole.

Confronting our pain

What surprised me most about my healing process was the way that God began to heal me. In the couple of months following my transformative experience with God, after I read Ezekiel 36:26, the Lord had been moving in my life to help me start to understand my brokenness and to open up emotionally.

Then I found out my uncle had passed away. He was cleaning a gun in his house, and it went off and hit him in the stomach. He died instantly. It was a shock. Ever since I'd known him as a kid, he was an incredibly strong dude. He was a Golden Glove boxer, a big, tall guy who was extremely muscular. But, over the last decade of his life, my uncle began having major back problems. It got to the point where doctors had to insert a morphine pump into his back. He became weak and was in constant pain, and that changed my uncle. Instead of being the tough guy who had always said, "Suck it up!" or "Don't show weakness" in the face of pain, he softened and became open and honest. The last time I saw him, my uncle actually gave me his Bible, and it was one of the first times I had an actual conversation with him.

Still, when I first heard he had died, I didn't really feel anything. I was worried because I had never responded emotionally to loss before. I had always been able to compartmentalize it. The Ezekiel 36 passage flowed through my mind, and I thought, *Am I too far gone? Can I just not feel anything anymore?*

I traveled to New Mexico to be with my aunt and cousins, and as I talked to them about my uncle, I started breaking down and crying. It was out of nowhere, and it was an interesting, cathartic experience. I had been so afraid to feel emotion, but after crying with them, I felt *good.* I realized that I cared about my uncle and about my family enough to feel pain *with* them. At that moment, I could sense that I was crying not only for what I was actually feeling about losing my uncle, but I was crying in an empathetic way toward what *they* were feeling.

I obviously had been under the impression that God would heal me and give me inner peace by covering over pain and trauma. What I didn't realize was that I didn't need God to become yet another coping mechanism to numb my pain. I needed Him to teach me how to confront my pain so I could properly heal.

As we learn to do this with the pain from our past, we also learn to deal with our present issues. After all, the Bible doesn't merely promise to help us get over our past hurts. It actually promises that we will be made better as a result of our past pain. Romans 5:3-5 declares, "And not only that, but we also glory in tribulations, knowing that tribulation produces perseverance; and perseverance, character; and character, hope. Now hope does not disappoint, because the love of God has been poured out in our hearts by the Holy Spirit who was given to us." (NKJV)

It is not that, as Christians, we want to suffer or are somehow grateful for trauma. But because of what Jesus has done for us, we can appreciate and even rejoice in what pain and trauma can produce within us. As wretched as my past pain is, I am thankful for what it has done in me and through me. If we had the ability to be fully numb to the past or even able to forget all about it, we would wall ourselves away from the unique greatness and beauty that God had stored for us in that pain. Our trauma is not meaningless, nor is our pain a waste of time. No matter how severe and horrid it is, it can be used by God to benefit us and help us grow in Him.

As God began to walk with me through my past trauma and present painful situations, He began to teach me how to confront my emotions instead of numbing myself to them. Despite all the coping mechanisms that caused me to run away from my emotions, I never had healing or experienced growth. I just became more deadened as my problems and disorders became worse. Only by confronting my emotions with God did I find healing in them. It was a very scary and often painful process, but as I learned to do this, I began to recover.

Not long after my uncle's death, I was researching some information on mental health when I stumbled across a writer and lecturer on psychology, politics, and the arts named Andrew Solomon who authored a book called *The Noonday Demon: An Atlas of Depression*. I found a TED Talk in which he described what depression felt like—and for the first time, I realized that I had suffered from depression, all the way back from the time of my skiing accident as a kid. I thought back to what I called my "periods of apathy" where I just didn't feel anything for weeks, sometimes months, at a time. I didn't want to be around people. I isolated myself and listened to depressing music. I didn't really understand what was wrong with me. I just did it.

As I recognized my almost lifelong struggle with depression, I didn't know what to do with it. Then, the following month, I listened to a sermon on Psalm 42. The pastor said the psalm was about someone with depression, and he went through it in such a way that it instructed me on how to communicate my emotions to God. After that, whenever I felt angry or sad, I started turning to the Psalms for guidance, and I developed a deep love for those 150 chapters in the middle of the Old Testament. They modeled how to go to God and immediately start talking to Him about what I was going through.

We need to learn to be honest in our communication with God. Since I always suppressed my pain and hurt, I lost the ability to be truthful with myself about what was really bothering me and candid about what I really needed. In every circumstance where I was hurting, I would usually make a joke out of it, then tell myself to suck it up and deal with my problems on my own. How could I possibly be honest with God if I couldn't even be honest with myself? To make matters worse, I had a cold relationship with God. I didn't think He really cared for me or even wanted to hear about my problems, but He showed me in His Word just how wrong I was.

Hebrews 4:15-16 reveals, "For we do not have a High Priest who cannot sympathize with our weaknesses, but was in all points tempted as we are, yet without sin. Let us therefore come boldly to the throne of grace, that we may obtain mercy and find grace to help in time of need." (NKJV) The phrase to "come boldly" literally means to have the freedom to say anything we want without fear. The writer of Hebrews was telling us that no matter what we are going through, Jesus can be sympathetic toward us and desires to hear what's sincerely on our heart. Remember, God wasn't immune to injustice or trauma, but entered into it willingly. Jesus was mocked, spat upon, betrayed, and murdered in one of the most brutal ways imaginable, and He didn't have to go through any of it. He chose to. Christ dwelled in the richness of His kingdom, immune to all forms of trauma, yet He willingly left His throne and lived a life filled with pain and suffering that ultimately led to His death.

The only One who was actually whole and unbroken became broken for you so that you might become whole in Him. When you understand the level of care and love that God has for you, it can enable you to start facing the hard truths—fear, pain, loneliness, or anything uncomfortable—that you have been running from for so long.

At the end of the Hebrews passage, it says we can come to God so that "we may obtain mercy and find grace to help in time of need." God desperately wants to help us in our pain, but He can't help unwilling people. We may think that we are being holy when we withhold our true feelings from God, especially those of doubt and anger, but we are actually pushing away the only One who can give us the actual help we need to grow and move past our pain.

Yet we also cannot try to force this kind of emotional honesty. It doesn't happen overnight. It takes time and determination to acquire and maintain emotional vulnerability and intimacy with God. We must be careful to not recklessly dig into old painful memories and try to manufacture pain or guess what is bothering us and then talk about these things with God. When I started counseling people with trauma as an associate pastor, I learned that most people lack the ability to compartmentalize pain. For them, digging up the past is not difficult, and they can't control their feelings. Because of that, they'd go back into their past and get stuck there, retraumatizing themselves as they ruminated and relived their trauma. In the end, that just made things worse for them.

We don't want to come to false conclusions about our issues and needs. We have to be patient with the process and understand that intimacy with God is supposed to be gentle and gradual, not instant. Once we know that we have the freedom to be honest with God, we need to consistently pour out our hearts before Him as we ponder and meditate over our trauma. We do this by trusting that God will slowly and systematically reveal what we are going through to us, and He will help us process these things with Him. We should pray as David did in Psalm 139. "Search me, O God, and know my heart; Try me, and know my anxieties; And see if there is any wicked way in me, And lead me in the way everlasting." (Psalm 139:23-24, NKJV)

Praying our emotions

Most of us are controlled by our emotions. They either overwhelm us and become the veil through which we view our reality, or we run from them and seek to suppress them. Either way, our emotions dictate our behavior and our actions.

Yet God doesn't want us to give in to our emotions and allow them to control us, but He doesn't want us to deny them, either. He wants us to learn to accept our emotions and wrestle with them, understanding that they are not bad in and of themselves, as some Christians falsely believe. There are many sections of the Bible that encourage us to experience our emotions. God Himself experiences emotions, and they are part of being made in His image and likeness. He's the reason we have emotions in the first place.

However, because of the mental issues we struggle with, our past pain, and our own sin, our emotions can easily go awry, so we need to learn how to appropriately deal with them. We must allow ourselves to feel and express our emotions, then seek comfort and help so we can cope with them when they are right and fight them when they are wrong.

The way Christians can do this with God is through prayer. For most believers in Jesus, prayer has unfortunately become a time where we just placidly ask for things. But when we look at the prayers spoken throughout the Bible, we discover that prayer is not that at all. Rather, prayer is more about expressing our deepest, most intimate feelings to God and seeking His correction and comfort in times of need. The Bible calls this type of prayer "meditation," but it isn't like meditation in eastern religions where one seeks to empty their mind. Biblical meditation involves thinking through our thoughts and emotions before God.

Look at the prayer Jesus taught His disciples in Matthew 6:9-13.

> Our Father in heaven,
> Hallowed be Your name.
> Your kingdom come.
> Your will be done
> On earth as it is in heaven.
> Give us this day our daily bread.
> And forgive us our debts,
> As we forgive our debtors.
> And do not lead us into temptation,
> But deliver us from the evil one.
> For Yours is the kingdom and the power and the glory forever. Amen. (NKJV)

Notice that the vast majority of it is not about asking for things. It is predominantly about meditating on God Himself and other key issues like confessing sin and seeking to forgive others. It's not that we shouldn't ask God for things. It's just that, primarily, we need to learn how to express ourselves to God in brutally honest ways that will enable Him to speak practically into our lives. The alternative is staying stuck in our own heads as our emotions rule over us.

One of the reasons our Western culture is one of the most stressed out and depressed civilizations that has ever existed, despite our incredible amounts of prosperity, is because we have too many distractions to be able to process the deeper things of the heart. Complex emotions and memories take a lot of time and mental focus to process. Beyond that, we have to remember that God is a person, not some impersonal power or force that is up there controlling the universe. He can be known in the same way we know and relate to an individual person. When we experience intimacy with a person, it requires giving that relationship time and attention. Unfortunately, our culture is so filled with constant mental stimulation, we never get time to be silent and press into God in prayer. Because of this, we never get around to processing what we are going through, leaving our emotions to insidiously control us and weigh on our minds and our hearts.

Sometimes we think that more input is the solution to our brokenness, so we read more books, listen to more sermons, and seek more counsel. But attempting to absorb too much keeps us from really absorbing anything at all. Perhaps this is why James 1:21-25 counsels us instead to "lay aside all filthiness and overflow of wickedness, and receive with meekness the implanted word, which is able to save your souls. But be doers of the word, and not hearers only, deceiving yourselves. For if anyone is a hearer of the word and not a doer, he is like a man observing his natural face in a mirror; for he observes himself, goes away, and immediately forgets what kind of man he was. But he who looks into the perfect law of liberty and continues in it, and is not a forgetful hearer but a doer of the work, this one will be blessed in what he does." (NKJV) If we never get around to really thinking through and applying what we are learning, it's all but forgotten before it can impact us.

As Christians, we need to evaluate our hearts and ask ourselves, "Do I know how to simply be *still* in the presence of God?" (Psalm 46:10) "Can I sit in silence and give myself time to process my thoughts and my emotions?" If we can't, our emotions will continue to control us. Yet cultivating this time of deep, intimate prayer with God is not an easy thing to do. I have been a Christian for almost all of my life, and it wasn't until very recently that I realized just how shallow my prayer life really was. It happened when I read Timothy Keller's book, *Prayer: Experiencing Awe and Intimacy with God*, which gives an in depth look at what prayer is all about. Keller commented that Christ's disciples had been believers in God ever since they were children because they were Jewish, yet when they listened to Jesus pray and saw His intimacy with the Father, they wanted Christ to teach them how to enter into that same level of intimacy with the Lord. Keller shared his own story of how he had been a pastor for years, but it wasn't until years later that he started praying the same thing the disciples did in Matthew 6 before Jesus delivered what we know as the Lord's Prayer: "God, teach me how to pray."

The good news is that growing your prayer life with God is just like developing intimacy with another person. True quality time and deep vulnerability don't come out of nowhere. They only come when you give a *quantity* of time and effort toward the relationship as a whole. The more time you spend pouring into another person, the safer you will feel with them—and that will, in turn, give you the freedom to begin sharing more intimate things with them.

God works the same way. We can't just start praying and expect our prayer lives to be instantly amazing. We have to be patient with growing our intimacy with God. This means setting aside a daily time just for prayer where we go to a quiet place free from distractions and seek Him. At first, our minds will wander and almost nothing deep or personal will come out. We cannot get discouraged by this but must continue being as honest and genuine with Him as we can. It can also be helpful to spend time journaling about our emotions as part of this daily intimacy with God. Remember, too, that this time with God is not so He can simply heal us and we can get on with our lives. We are striving above all else to get closer to Him. Healing may be a fruit that comes from this time, but knowing God Himself is the goal.

Another great way to develop your intimacy with God is to read through the Psalms, review some of the prayers of Old Testament prophets like Jeremiah in the book of Lamentations, and read through the prayers of biblical personalities like Daniel, Micah, and Elijah. My favorite book of the Bible is Jeremiah. His prayer life ministered to me because he clearly struggled through depression. I deeply connected with the things he said and the metaphors he used in his prayers. We also see in Jeremiah how the Lord responded to His prophet and how God's counsel for him shifted depending on what Jeremiah needed at the moment. Sometimes God was stern. Other times, He was very gentle. It shows God being a wonderful counselor to Jeremiah and maneuvering in his life.

In addition, Lamentations is incredible. Also written by Jeremiah, the entire book is prayer, five chapters of really personal, intimate stuff. Not too many people read it because of how vulnerable it is. Jeremiah did not put on a spiritual front that he was doing okay. He poured out raw, unfiltered emotion before God, sometimes blatantly accusing God of failing him and His people. Reading through Jeremiah will help you better understand the context since Lamentations was written in a singular moment toward the end of his ministry when he was incarcerated, and his beloved city of Jerusalem was in flames. You'll discover that Jeremiah had been prophesying for decades and had faced hatred and animosity as well as being thrown into prison. It was written by a man who spent his entire life trying to reach his community, only to watch them taken over by the enemy because they did not heed his words.

Perhaps most interesting of all is the fact that Jeremiah was never healed from his depression. I can relate to that. When you get to the end of the book of Jeremiah, his life is much harder, yet he is steadfast. That is why Lamentations 3:21-25 is one of my favorite passages in all of the Bible: "Yet this I call to mind and therefore I have hope: Because of the Lord's great love we are not consumed, for his compassions never fail. They are new every morning; great is your faithfulness. I say to myself, "The Lord is my portion; therefore I will wait for him." It is a declaration of faith and hope that gives me a lot of confidence. I may not ever stop feeling depressed, but I can get to the place that Jeremiah did where my emotions no longer control me, and I can learn to express them the way he did.

That's genuine prayer. But when we learn how to pray from example, such as before a meal or when a pastor prays before a church service, prayer is usually modeled as something we have to get through in order to get to something better. Reading through the prayers in the Bible shows us what prayer is intended to be. The saints of old longed to be in the presence of God. They loved being in that quiet place with their Lord, and they always looked forward to speaking with Him.

If this type of longing for God in prayer is foreign to you, that's okay. It's pretty normal. But the more you seek to grow your prayer life, the more God will meet you right where you are and help you cultivate an active and dynamic prayer life with Him. In the end, the closer you get to God in your daily prayer life, the more He will be able to counsel you through your brokenness.

As we learn to grow in intimacy with God through honest expression, we also need to renew our minds and our thoughts through His perfect truth found in the Bible. Once we begin to sit in silence with God, it is imperative that we learn how to listen to God. Most Christians think that "hearing" from God is something that only happens to incredibly spiritual people as He speaks to them in an audible voice. While that can happen, the primary method He uses to communicate with us is His inspired Word. When we go to the pages of the Bible, we aren't simply reading a book. We are reading the very revelation of God Himself.

If reading Scripture has become a cold, routine act for you, it might be because you have been approaching the pages of the Bible out of intellectual curiosity or religious obligation. For years, I didn't see the Bible as a means of becoming more intimate with God, but simply as an old book that I was "supposed" to read. I was mainly bored and didn't get much out of it. But as my intimacy with God began to develop in a quiet place of prayer, I began to approach reading the Scripture not as an obligation, but as a joy. I started to see the Bible as a means to hear from God, to understand Him in a more intimate way, and as the primary way to understand His desires—and that, for me, was in dealing with my emotions.

Emotions are powerful and persuasive. Unless we are renewing our minds in His truth, we can never develop the faith necessary to manage our emotions. I'll get more into how this looks later, but for now understand that praying our emotions brings us into a place of intimacy with God, and it is in this intimate place that we become ready to hear from God as His Spirit helps us understand, experience, and believe His truth above our emotions.

It is also in this time of prayer that we can learn how to gently press into our past pain and hurt, confront it, feel it, and deal with it. Some people think they can experience healing faster if they "bravely" dig into all their past pain and deal with it all at once. Therapists call this "flooding" or immersion therapy, and it usually has an adverse effect on the healing process. Instead of getting better, it usually causes more trauma and makes the wounds worse. What they recommend now is *progressive* immersion. For example, when dealing with someone who has a fear of heights, maybe they can first go to a room on the upper floor in a building, then walk toward the balcony and gradually to the railing. Slow, progressive steps are taken to address the fear instead of immersing them in it all at once. The idea is to take something small but doable, then slowly take it a little farther so they get accustomed to that feeling of fear. For most people with PTSD, once their brain marks something as being traumatic, it will almost always stay that way, but they can learn to get used to that feeling and discover how to control it so it doesn't control them.

Prayer is a type of progressive therapy with God. Instead of trying to dive into our deepest most painful memories in a singular moment, we develop closeness and intimacy with the Lord as He gradually enables us to confront our past and deal with it over time. We discover that healing from mental wounds is not like "ripping off a Band-Aid," but is instead a slow process that needs to be approached with gentleness and patience—and it all begins by cultivating a deep, personal prayer life with God.

Why are you cast down, O my soul? And why are you disquieted within me?
Hope in God, for I shall yet praise Him for the help of His countenance.
Psalm 42:5, NKJV

Another reason why we need to begin to pray our emotions and deal with them is that refusing to do so will lead to what the Bible calls "a broken spirit." (Proverbs 18:14) In the Hebrew (one of the two original languages the Bible was written in, along with Greek), the word "spirit" or *ruach* was a very broad term that covered a large number of different contexts. It could reference the spiritual, immaterial world as opposed to the physical, material world. It may also mean breath, wind, or power. It could allude to the position of our emotional vitality and strength.

In Proverbs 18, the spirit was seen as being like a muscle responsible for our emotional well-being. So, to have a "broken spirit" was to have the "muscle" that regulates our emotional strength be torn and useless.

When you feel broken in this way, you are dried up and empty emotionally. You feel hollow, as if you are cut off from everyone and everything around you. Being in this state makes you feel like everything is far away and that life itself is distant, leaving you aimless and utterly alone within it. It seems as if everything requires too much effort. Even the simplest tasks are burdensome to you, robbed of all of their former pleasure and joy. You find it difficult to get up in the morning or communicate with anyone. It is even a chore to eat and take care of yourself.

This brokenness leads to incredible amounts of emotional instability. Proverbs 25:28 warns, "Whoever has no rule over his own spirit Is like a city broken down, without walls." (NKJV) What this means is that your spirit acts as a protector over your emotional state, just as walls served to protect ancient cities. To have "no rule" over your spirit prevents your spirit from performing its primary function. This leaves your heart vulnerable to whatever emotion comes around. People in this state tend to disproportionately overreact. The smallest thing can set them off, the tiniest amount of sadness can bring them to tears, the smallest amount of stress can send them into a panic attack, and the barest hint of anger can cause them to blow up on someone. Remember when I got angry with my friends on the military base in California? I blew up then because I had never really dealt with my emotions, so my spirit was incredibly weak and incapable of controlling my emotional state. My reaction then was kind of the result of a broken spirit, but not fully. It was more the result of me not having yet trained my spirit.

My spirit had become broken because I sealed it up and refused to use it. Whenever I felt emotions, I cut myself off from them, pretending they weren't there. I did this so often and so well that it came naturally and without effort. Locking my spirit in a box caused it to atrophy to the point where it no longer functioned properly. That's why I constantly felt numb, and I couldn't confront even the simplest of problems. It completely arrested my emotional development and made it impossible for me to confront or deal with any of my past pain. I was only able to bury it, unable to deal with what was bothering me in a healthy or productive way.

The main overarching cause of a broken spirit, the muscle that regulates our emotions, is its overuse. When we go through trauma, our spirit works overtime to help us process the flood of extreme emotions that come our way. When we experience intense loss, grief, stress, or anger, whether due to the extreme nature of what we are going through or its long duration, our spirit can become overburdened and break under the extreme weight it is carrying.

This condition can become even more harmful when someone with a broken spirit tries to function as if everything is normal. It's like walking on a broken leg. You might be able to walk a short distance, but every step you take is causing more damage to your already injured body.

The good news is that having a broken spirit isn't a terminal illness. The spirit can be revitalized, but just like an injured muscle, it takes time and therapy. You may have to take a step back from your day-to-day obligations and give your spirit time to absorb what it needs to process so you can move forward through the pain. This doesn't necessarily mean you quit your job and drop all of your responsibilities, but it does mean you need to possibly start cutting some things out and take a break from your duties. Of course, simply resting a broken bone isn't enough to repair it. You must also slowly exercise it as it heals; otherwise, the bone will not properly mend.

Praying your emotions is a form of exercise for your spirit that allows it to engage emotions gradually and in the safety of your Father's presence. This strengthens your spirit so that it can do its job and enable you to experience emotions without being ruled by them. Be patient with this process. It will take time for your spirit to heal. Don't be discouraged if at first you don't feel anything, or if you feel so much that you want to give up. You're likely not far enough along in your healing to process your emotions quite yet. Instead, work on journaling and meditating on any small emotions that you feel throughout the day. Maintain your relationships instead of isolating. Keep asking God to reveal His truth to you so that you can better understand your emotional state. Stay steadfast in prayer while gently pushing yourself to talk about your emotions with those who are helping you in this healing process.

As you are patient, God will begin to mend your broken spirit and bring emotional vitality.

Comfort in sorrow

The first emotion God taught me to express was sorrow. I had always hated feeling sad, especially in front of other people. I had always seen sadness as a weakness, so I never let myself feel it. But doing that made me cold and bitter in the end. God had to teach me how to feel my sorrow and to learn to express that sadness to Him. The Bible refers to this as sowing tears (Psalm 126:5). It enables us to actually grow as a result of the pain that we have been through as opposed to being numbed to it.

Again, Jeremiah was key as I learned how to do this. He wrote in Jeremiah 9:1, "Oh, that my head were a spring of water and my eyes a fountain of tears! I would weep day and night for the slain of my people." (NIV) Whenever Jeremiah felt intense sorrow, he didn't run away from those emotions or attempt to distract himself from them. Instead, he committed himself to go to God and express his hurt so he might have comfort in his time of need. When we are able to feel our emotions like this with God, He then has the opportunity to draw closer to us and provide His comfort.

Think about the relationship between a parent and a child. The first and most powerful form of bonding that happens in that relationship is when a parent learns to comfort their crying child. Those early moments when a baby only knows how to cry out when in need bring an incredible amount of unity and trust between parent and child. That's the kind of intimacy we are encouraged to have with our heavenly Father. Romans 8:15 declares that we "have received the Spirit of adoption by whom we cry out, 'Abba, Father.'" (NKJV) It's been said the Hebrew word *abba* is actually closer to our English word "daddy" than it is to "dad" or "father."

But I think we can take that one step further. *Abba* is actually closest to "dadda." The two words even sound alike. "Dadda" infers a special type of intimacy because it is usually the way infants first cry out to their father. So, Paul, who in Romans 8 is talking to Christians going through severe suffering, encourages those believers to come to God and "cry out" in the same desperate, loving way an infant cries for its parents.

That is why sorrow came first for me. Crying out like a child didn't require a deep understanding of my emotional state. It didn't even necessitate words. I just needed vulnerability, a willingness to feel deep sorrow, and a desire to be comforted in that still, quiet place by God.

It is this kind of intimacy and closeness that God desires to have with His children, and sorrow can be the mechanism to get us there. That doesn't mean we should be whiners before God, but if we legitimately feel pain, we can invite Him into our suffering by expressing that pain, so He is able to comfort us. This results in amazing amounts of unity and closeness between us and God as we learn to trust Him more and more. As that trust grows, we will start to feel the freedom to not only express current pain to God, but to begin gently digging into our past pain and experiencing comfort that will heal those old wounds.

In His famous Sermon on the Mount, Jesus gives a precious promise, saying that those who mourn will be comforted. Christ does not say He will take away our sorrow, but that He will comfort us *in* our sorrow. Some Christians who come to God with their sorrow feel like He has ignored them because He didn't take away their sadness. But receiving His comfort in sorrow isn't the same as numbing our sorrow. It involves experiencing intimacy, sympathy, and understanding as we are sorrowful. This eventually allows us to be lifted out of our sorrow stronger and closer to God than we ever were before, which is a far greater blessing than feeling nothing at all. This comfort is offered only to those who mourn, not to those who ignore or bury their sadness. We can never experience the blessed comfort offered to us by our loving Father if we suppress our feelings or lie about our hurt.

This is a very important lesson to learn when we want to comfort someone else. When another person is hurting, what they need most is not a profound answer or a solution to their problems. They simply need you to be present. If you've never learned how to be comforted, all you will be able to offer those who are hurting is a brief distraction or a small piece of advice. True intimacy occurs when you are able to sit with someone in their sadness and experience their pain as if it were your own. Learning to receive comfort so you can then, in turn, comfort others is essential in developing unity in the midst of shared suffering (2 Corinthians 1:3-5).

This was so tough for me to do. Early on, everything in me cried out to numb my emotions and run away from my feelings. But God desires us to experience sorrow just as He did. Isaiah 53:4-5 reveals, "Surely He has borne our griefs And carried our sorrows; Yet we esteemed Him stricken, Smitten by God, and afflicted. But He was wounded for our transgressions, He was bruised for our iniquities; The chastisement for our peace was upon Him, and by His stripes we are healed." (NKJV)

After reading this and understanding that it was speaking of Jesus Christ and His death on the cross, I asked myself, "If God was willing to experience pain without numbing Himself to draw near to me, am I willing to experience pain without numbing myself to draw near to Him?" It is not a strength to not feel anything. It is apathy produced by cowardice. True strength is being able to feel the depths of our pain without numbing ourselves or breaking under its pressure. This brings us deep into the arms of our Savior, and it is in His arms that we will be "hard-pressed on every side, yet not crushed; we are perplexed, but not in despair; persecuted, but not forsaken; struck down, but not destroyed." (2 Corinthians 4:8-9, NKJV)

Bitterness toward God

As I began to express my sorrow to God, something unexpected happened. He began to reveal a great amount of hurt and bitterness that I harbored toward Him. When we think back to our past trauma, it is completely natural to ask the question, "If God loved me so much, why did He let that happen to me?" I carried that hurt for years, but because I was a "good Christian" who refused to express any doubt or frustration with God because to do so was a sign of faithlessness or sin, I was never able to admit to myself that I felt that way. But as I learned to express my disappointment and sadness to God, He began to show me the truth of my emotions and give me the strength to admit those feelings to Him.

I also found that I was not alone in the way I felt as I studied God's Word. The writer of Psalm 42:9 said, "I will say to God my Rock, 'Why have You forgotten me? Why do I go mourning because of the oppression of the enemy?'" When we read through the Bible, we discover that many great men of faith like Job, Jeremiah, Elijah, David, and others expressed things like this to God. They didn't hide their feelings in fear of God; instead, they told their raw, unedited emotions to Him because they understood the great love that God had for them. We need to learn how to do the same. Unless we do, we will, at best, cover over our feelings of hurt and never really deal with them. At worst, our bitterness will overwhelm us, and we will curse God and leave Him.

This process is sometimes made worse by the fact that other Christians are quick to react and tell us not to think, much less say, such things to the Lord. Sadly, Christians tend to offer weak, superficial expressions of hope to try to address gaping wounds. When someone expresses pain over how God could allow something horrible to happen, well-meaning believers in Jesus will say things such as, "God is in control," or "They are in a better place now." C.S. Lewis was a famous Christian author who had someone try to comfort him by saying he shouldn't be sad after his wife died because she was "in God's hands." In his book, *A Grief Observed,* Lewis journaled his emotions and responded to that attempt at "comfort."

He wrote, "'Because she is in God's hands.' But if so, she was in God's hands all the time, and I have seen what they did to her here. Do they suddenly become gentler to us the moment we are out of the body? And if so, why? If God's goodness is inconsistent with hurting us, then either God is not good or there is no God: for in the only life we know He hurts us beyond our worst fears and beyond all we can imagine. If it is consistent with hurting us, then He may hurt us after death as unendurably as before it."

It may seem odd to read something like that from such a great man of faith as C.S. Lewis, but don't miss the point. First of all, emotional wounds cut deeper than physical ones and take longer than physical wounds to heal. When someone is hurting, we shouldn't offer cheap answers, but mourn with them and comfort them. There will be time to help people understand God's love in the midst of mourning, but more than anything, we simply need to be there for those who are hurting instead of trying to "fix" the situation. We are, as Romans 12:15 exhorts, to "rejoice with those who rejoice, weep with those who weep." (ESV)

For those of us who are hurting, this should also give us grace and patience for those who are trying to comfort us. I discovered early on in my healing process that the people I confided in often gave me bad advice or didn't know how to properly comfort me. My first instinct was to pull away from these people and even rage against them, but over time, I realized that while they didn't know how to properly help me, they were at least trying. It is awkward when people don't know what to say or how to act around those who are hurting, but the more I began to appreciate people's attempts, misguided as they were, I began to find comfort in their presence and their love, even if they lacked the wisdom to properly console me. I learned to be gentle with them and explain to them what was helpful to me and what was hurtful. This helped them grow in their ability to comfort, and it allowed me to develop relationships with those around me, producing strong, mutual support between me and those closest to me.

Pain and suffering are massively complex issues in the Bible. That's why there is no simple, concrete answer to the question of why bad things happen to us. All we can know for sure is that God is in control of this world, but because it is fallen, God allows evil things to occur for His purposes. This truth might frustrate us, but we can look to the cross for a reason to trust God even when pain is allowed into our lives.

The crucifixion of Jesus Christ was the most unjust and horrendous event in history, yet that shameful murder of the only innocent man to ever live was permitted and ordained by God. The triune God (Father, Son, and Holy Spirit) chose to taste death for us and experienced suffering in the process. Imagine the intense trauma the Father and the Holy Spirit had to endure when giving up the Son to be tortured and killed, or the pain the Son had to willingly feel as He was stripped naked, whipped, and crucified. But it was through this suffering that salvation and healing was made possible for all who would put their faith in God. When I accept that, I can believe, even though I don't fully understand, that if God can allow and use that horrible event to deliver us, then whatever trauma I have faced wasn't meaningless, but has a purpose.

Paul wrote in 2 Corinthians 4:17, "For our light affliction, which is but for a moment, is working for us a far more exceeding and eternal weight of glory, while we do not look at the things which are seen, but at the things which are not seen. For the things which are seen are temporary, but the things which are not seen are eternal." (NKJV) We are not to look at the trauma we can see, but trust in God's faithfulness and look to His purpose that can't be seen. We are able to have this faith because we know that we serve a God who showed us His faithfulness by suffering and dying for us. No wonder Romans 8:31-32 declares, "What then shall we say to these things? If God is for us, who can be against us? He who did not spare His own Son, but delivered Him up for us all, how shall He not with Him also freely give us all things?" (NKJV)

In the April 12, 2004 issue of Time magazine, the question was asked, "Why Did Jesus Have To Die?" Joanne Marie Terrell, author of the book *Power in the Blood? The Cross in the African American Experience*, was interviewed, and it was explained how the truth of Jesus' death gave her a way to cope with and even grow from the tragedy of witnessing her own mother being murdered. Several years ago, while sitting in a seminary class, Joanne had a flashback to when she was a girl, and her mother had just been murdered by her boyfriend. She saw the blood-soaked mattress and her mother's bloody handprint on the wall. Suddenly, she had to find a connection between her mom's story, her own story, and Jesus' story.

Terrell said the Christ connecting those stories was not just the one whose death had delivered her from sin. He was also the Christ who generations of African Americans had believed suffered with them as well as for them. Terrell realized that Jesus had stood by her in her pain, enabled her to see her mother as having died standing up to her abuser, and helped her find her place as a person living for God. She concluded that Christ's death was not only substitutionary, but He was also the one who truly identified with us in suffering and could provide an example of how to live our lives.

The more we allow the truth of Jesus' suffering to penetrate our hearts, the more we can see our past trauma as something that draws us to Christ instead of pushing us away from Him. When this intimacy happens, we can believe that God is with us not as a calloused observer, but as One who suffers with us and sympathizes with our pain, and also uses it for our good and His glory and as our source of healing. He will become to us the God spoken of in Isaiah 61:3 who consoles "those who mourn in Zion, To give them beauty for ashes, The oil of joy for mourning, The garment of praise for the spirit of heaviness; That they may be called trees of righteousness, The planting of the Lord, that He may be glorified." (NKJV) The beauty Isaiah promised isn't in spite of the ashes. It comes directly from the ashes. As long as shame about our past holds us captive, we will always be in bondage to our trauma. But when we accept this truth, it can silence the shame of our past and bring us to a place where we are no longer merely coping with our past, but we are growing as a result of it.

In the book of Genesis, we meet Joseph, a man who underwent incredible amounts of suffering and trauma at the hands of his own family. He was hated by his brothers because of the favoritism that his father showed to him. Their bitterness was so great that they kidnapped Joseph and sold him into slavery. Joseph spent years in bondage and in prison through no fault of his own. Yet throughout all of his suffering, Joseph clung to God for comfort and strength. Although he didn't have anyone else, God alone brought him through his trials. After Joseph was delivered from prison and became a prominent ruler in Egypt, he had two sons who he named Ephraim and Manasseh. "Joseph called the name of the firstborn Manasseh: 'For God has made me to forget all my toil and all my father's house.' And the name of the second he called Ephraim: 'For God has caused me to be fruitful in the land of my affliction.'" (Genesis 41:51-52, NKJV)

In Hebrew, "Manasseh" literally means "to forget," but it wasn't that God erased Joseph's memory and gave him amnesia. We know from the rest of the story that Joseph still remembered what happened to him and was moved to tears multiple times when he eventually saw his family again. The significance of the name's meaning is that Joseph forgot the labor caused by his past. Those who have experienced trauma know how our memories carry with them a great deal of toil. They are emotionally taxing and incredibly burdensome, bearing all of our triggers, shame, and internal scars. But when Joseph thought back to all those memories, the trauma, anxiety, and humiliation from what he had been through were completely gone.

The name of his second child, Ephraim, means "fruitful" in Hebrew. This fruitfulness that Joseph encountered wasn't in spite of what he had been through, but because of the prosperity he saw in the very midst of his trials. Later in Genesis, we are told that Ephraim received a double portion blessing from his grandfather, signifying that Joseph's fruitfulness outweighed God's work to help him forget his past toil. When the Lord brought prosperity in Joseph's life, it came directly from his trial, and that prosperity was so great that God's miraculous work of taking away the pain of his past was more insignificant to Joseph than God's work of causing his prosperity to descend from his trauma. As a result, Joseph experienced Post-Traumatic Growth through the comfort of God.

He had to wait years before he saw the fruit of his affliction, but he trusted in God's faithfulness. Truth is, some of us may never see the fruit that comes from our pain, but if we can accept God's role in it, we can also experience growth that comes directly from our trauma.

For me, the idea that my suffering had purpose was one of the biggest keys to my healing. When I first came back home from Afghanistan, I looked at all my past suffering and shrugged my shoulders, saying "Life is tough. I have to get over this." But no matter how often I told myself this, it didn't change the fact that I was eaten up with anger over what had happened to me. After all my friends and I had been through, I couldn't help looking back on all of it and saying, "What was it all for? Everything is worse now." That frustration and shame about my trauma locked me within my pain to where I thought I had no hope of escape.

It wasn't until I began to recognize the purpose behind my suffering that I was able to not just accept what happened to me, but to derive hope from it. In the hands of God, our trauma will produce something beautiful. I am certainly not happy about what I went through, but I see God's involvement in it and believe that just as the Father turned His own Son's suffering into glory, He can do the same for me.

In the time I have been sharing my story, I've had the ability to relate to so many hurt people on such an intimate level. As difficult as my past was, I am actually thankful for what I have suffered, and I know that far more fruit is even now being prepared for me by my Father. Joni Eareckson Tada is a woman who suffered an accident that made her a quadriplegic. Here is what she said about her suffering:

"Most of us are able to thank God for His grace, comfort, and sustaining power in a trial, but we don't thank Him for the problem, just finding Him in it. But many decades in a wheelchair have taught me to not segregate my Savior from the suffering He allows, as though a broken neck—or, in your case, a broken ankle, heart, or home—merely 'happens' and then God shows up after the fact to wrestle something good out of it. No, the God of the Bible is bigger than that. Much bigger. And so is the capacity of your soul."

"Maybe this wheelchair felt like a horrible tragedy in the beginning, but I give God thanks in my wheelchair. I'm grateful for my quadriplegia. It's a bruising of a blessing. A gift wrapped in black. It's the shadowy companion that walks with me daily, pulling and pushing me into the arms of my Savior. And that's where the joy is ... Your "wheelchair," whatever it is, falls well within the overarching decrees of God. Your hardship and heartache come from His wise and kind hand, and, for that, you can be grateful. In it and for it."[iii]

Blessed are those who mourn, For they shall be comforted.
Matthew 5:4, NKJV

Chapter 6
Healing in Forgiveness

As I began to trust God in my pain and believe in His love for me in my suffering, I learned that I needed to forgive those who had hurt me. To those who have been abused and traumatized, that may sound bizarre, but that is likely because we don't fully understand what forgiveness is and why we do it. Most people tend to think that forgiving someone means letting go of their anger and getting over what was done to them. But there is far more to it than that.

Psalm 37:8 tells us to "cease from anger, and forsake wrath; do not fret—it only causes harm." (NKJV) The first thing I needed to see was the unbelievable damage my own anger was doing to me. Because of the way our emotions work, feeding our anger actually roots us deeper in our trauma. If we ever want to have any hope of truly healing from it, we must forgive and give our anger to God. If we are unable to do that, our anger will only get worse as we constantly think about our past injustices and become further entrenched in our pain.

I also discovered that the angrier I got, the more that anger would spill over onto the people closest to me. Even though I didn't intend for that to happen, I became a wrathful and bitter person who could not control my temper. It became very easy for me to go from zero to 100 in an argument, making me vindictive, judgmental, and petty. I expressed all of my negative emotions as anger, and I used apathy and anger as coping mechanisms to deal with my more undesirable emotions like sadness and fear. Whenever I felt unhappy or afraid, instead of vulnerably confessing those emotions to those around me and asking for their help and comfort, I got mad and pushed people away in my wrath. This kept all of my relationships at length because I was never able to invite other people into my suffering.

As a result, all of my relationships became superficial. To develop intimacy, relationships need emotional honesty and vulnerability, but I was unable to give either one. No matter how sincerely people wanted to help, they couldn't keep reaching out to me when I attacked them simply for trying to get too close. Deep down, there was a part of me that just wanted to be left alone and didn't feel like I deserved to have people care. Basically, I pushed them away before they could leave me first. I would alienate myself in my anger and then complain that I was alone. I even blamed others for not reaching out to me enough. Bitterness is a poison that only brings destruction and isolation.

I also lacked peace in my life. As I sulked in my anger, I couldn't help but constantly think about all the people who had wronged me. I ruminated over past conversations and events and imagined what I wished I would have said or done differently. I started noticing this tendency while I was still in the Marines. I recall one time, between my two deployments, when I was stopped by a military police officer as I was driving on base. That annoyed me since in the military a traffic violation doesn't result in a fine, but in a loss of three points on your driving record. A loss of 12 points meant loss of license—but I had zero points against me, and I was going to deploy again in a week. The three points simply wouldn't matter. I told this to the officer, but he didn't care. I was so mad, I just kept smiling at him in a sarcastic and disrespectful manner as he wrote out the violation. It was a small thing, almost insignificant, but it was those kinds of incidents that I'd ruminate about over and over.

I became stuck in my own head—until I finally realized that my anger had overcome me.

But even then, I was still unwilling to forgive until God showed me the truth about forgiveness.

Ephesians 4:32 tells us, "Be kind to one another, tenderhearted, forgiving one another, even as God in Christ forgave you." (NKJV) God brought this passage to me as I wrestled with the anger, bitterness, and resentment I'd harbored for years. As I realized I needed to forgive others the same way God forgave me, it finally clicked. Did God simply wave His hand over my sin and say, "Don't worry about it. It's no big deal?" No way! God was so serious about judging my sin that He had to die to pay the price for what I had done. Forgiveness isn't about excusing someone else's actions or "letting things go." It's about giving God the authority to judge so that you don't have to.

What do I mean by that? Some of us believe that we have already forgiven those who have hurt us in the past, or we conclude that we have no need to forgive those in our past because we have tricked ourselves into thinking that we don't feel any more anger toward them. We know it's the "Christian" thing to forgive, and because we accept it is wrong to be bitter, we convince ourselves that we have already completely forgiven those who have wronged us. It could be that we just don't want to think about our past or risk giving the person who hurt us the satisfaction of knowing that we were damaged by what they did. So, when we say things like, "I'm over it" or "it is what it is," it has more to do with convincing ourselves than convincing others. In reality, all we have done is suppressed our anger toward others and allowed that wound to fester to the point our bitterness is poured out on those around us.

Then there are those times when we know that we should forgive but think that to forgive means to forget, so we refuse to do so because we don't want to forget. That would allow the other person to get away with what they did, so we hold on to our anger in an attempt to get back at them. When we routinely lose control and overreact but don't know why, it is probably because we have suppressed the cause of our anger, leaving us with bitterness and frustration. This can be especially true when dealing with events—such as the death of a loved one or the loss of property from a crime or natural disaster—where there isn't a person to forgive. In those cases, we must learn to accept that the event happened, then forgive the event itself by handing over our anger about it to the Lord, trusting the promise of Romans 8:28 that, somehow, "all things work together for good to those who love God, to those who are the called according to His purpose."

In order to have healing in forgiveness, you need to admit that you are angry, see the wrong that happened to you, acknowledge that what happened deserves justice—and then *give* the right of that vengeance over to God.

Even those who admit they were wronged and clearly understand why they are so angry can refuse to forgive because they want to judge those who hurt them and make them pay. But we are terrible judges for several reasons. First, we already have so much sin in our lives, we have no right to judge others. As Proverbs 20:9 questions, "Who can say, 'I have made my heart clean, I am pure from my sin?'" (NKJV) Second, we lack the knowledge necessary to judge people in total fairness by taking into account their past and other extenuating circumstances. Finally, we do not have the authority to judge others as much as is needed. In other words, the most we have the power to do is kill someone. God, on the other hand, has not only the authority to take someone's life, but He is the only One in position to judge that person's soul for eternity. Matthew 10:28 rightly states, "Do not fear those who kill the body but cannot kill the soul. But rather fear Him who is able to destroy both soul and body in hell." (NKJV)

When we forgive someone who hurt us, they aren't getting away with anything. Instead, we are the ones who will be saved from the pain of our own wrath as we allow God to judge them in His righteousness. This causes us to humbly accept that they will find forgiveness at the cross, just as we have for the evil things we have done, and if they do, God will still discipline them for what they did. He will deal with them as His children in an attempt to help them change and come closer to Him, or they will stand before God one day and be judged without mercy. Either way, the authority is His, not ours. That's why Proverbs 20:22 exhorts, "Do not say, 'I will recompense evil'; Wait for the Lord, and He will save you." (NKJV)

How do we practically give our anger over to God? This process isn't easy or quick, but we are given a great example of what to do in Psalm 58:6-10. It says, "Break their teeth in their mouth, O God! Break out the fangs of the young lions, O Lord! Let them flow away as waters which run continually; When he bends his bow, Let his arrows be as if cut in pieces. Let them be like a snail which melts away as it goes, Like a stillborn child of a woman, that they may not see the sun. Before your pots can feel the burning thorns, He shall take them away as with a whirlwind, As in His living and burning wrath. The righteous shall rejoice when he sees the vengeance; He shall wash his feet in the blood of the wicked." (NKJV)

This Psalm is one of the imprecatory, or cursing, Psalms. There are a couple of these in the Bible where the psalmists bring their wrath before God and express their desire to see justice done to those who have wronged them. Notice that they aren't seeking justice themselves. Instead, they are saying to God, "If I were you, this is what I would do." Yet they also recognize they aren't God, so they submit to God's justice.

I began this process by simply trying to daily forgive people for the wrongs that they had done to me. But because I had buried my past hurts so successfully that I couldn't really tell what I was angry about anymore, I also couldn't even specifically remember how I had been hurt to begin with. Therefore, I wrongly assumed that I had already forgiven those who had harmed me in my past.

However, I discovered that it was really hard for me to forgive even the simple wrongs that were being committed against me in the present by those closest to me. I began to see that there was a kind of invisible string that attached the current wrongs to all the past wrongs that I was trying so hard to forget. So, while the people in my present weren't nearly as damaging or hurtful as those from my past, the pain I was feeling toward them reminded me at some level of the trauma from my past. It revealed the true pain that I had covered over for so long, and it showed me that I had never truly forgiven those from my past like I thought I had. I had merely buried my resentment toward them deep down in my soul.

As I asked God to reveal the source of the bitterness in my heart, I began the process of discovering true and genuine forgiveness toward those in my past and my present. That in turn started to set me free from all of my built-up anger and hostility.

When you begin doing this, you'll discover that as you try to forgive your spouse for belittling your emotions, you'll find out you also need to forgive the parent who beat you down emotionally as a child. When you try to forgive your boss for yelling at you, you'll see you are also forgiving others who abused you in the past. When you try to forgive your friend for breaking a promise, you'll also have to forgive that other person who cheated on you or abandoned you. This is why forgiveness can be so very difficult to give. It isn't just about forgiving what's happening right now. You also have to forgive what happened in the past.

I also learned that my reality wasn't the same as my anger made it out to be. For example, I made everyone who hurt me out to be the enemy and myself as the innocent victim. Yet as I brought these prayers to God, He showed me that I wasn't as blameless as I thought, and they weren't as guilty as I believed. The Lord began to help me see that I bore at least a little bit of the blame for what had happened in every situation. This may not be true for those who went through abuse that wasn't their fault at all. But for me, I realized that I was partially to blame for everything I struggled with. I also realized that I had made people out to be monsters devoid of any excuse or any redeemable quality. In my anger, I distorted them, assuming the worst about their actions and their intentions when, in reality, they simply weren't the demons that I portrayed them to be. Proverbs 19:11 reminds us that "the discretion of a man makes him slow to anger, And his glory is to overlook a transgression." (NKJV)

People are more complicated. There isn't anyone who is pure evil or pure good. Some might be more consumed by the sin in their hearts than others, but we are all made in the image of God. There is good in us, and we are capable of redemption and change through Christ. At the same time, we are fallen, which makes our very nature sinful and capable of great evil.

It made it easier for me to fight a war in Afghanistan when I pretended that everyone I was battling were evil and undeserving of sympathy or mercy. Yet over time, I saw they were people just like me. They were in a far different situation and culture, but I saw demonstrations of genuine goodness and genuine evil there just as I would in the United States or anywhere else. No matter how heinous someone's actions might be, they were not beyond the grace and love of God. The more I accepted this, the more I was enabled to forgive those who wronged me while trusting in His perfect justice.

Forgiving and being forgiven
Learning to forgive others is essential to receiving forgiveness. Matthew 6:14-15 teaches, "For if you forgive men their trespasses, your heavenly Father will also forgive you. But if you do not forgive men their trespasses, neither will your Father forgive your trespasses." (NKJV) There is a direct correlation between giving forgiveness and receiving it.

This passage does not say it is impossible to receive forgiveness from God unless you first give *perfect* forgiveness, for no one can honestly do that. Rather, Jesus said this in the midst of His Sermon on the Mount, specifically given to show the perfect standards of God, so we can see we can never reach those standards (or attain relationship with God the Father) without the sacrifice of the Son. However, once we receive Jesus as our Savior, we have to take His words seriously because, while we will never perfectly keep those words, they are the standard Jesus empowers us to emulate through His Spirit. That's why Jesus says, in the same sermon, "Therefore you shall be perfect, just as your Father in heaven is perfect." (Matthew 5:48, NKJV)

When we refuse to go through the painful process of forgiveness toward others, we become harsh and judgmental. This critical and abrasive mentality doesn't stop with how we view those who have hurt us, but it bleeds into our other relationships as we brutally condemn any behavior in our friends and family that reminds us of those who have wounded us. This can make us paranoid, hypercritical, and untrusting of others. It also carries over into the way we view ourselves. If we can't forgive a particular sin in someone else, how are we going to receive forgiveness when we see the exact same sin in our own lives? Most of us fall deep into denial and refuse to see such things in ourselves. This causes us to blame others in order to excuse our bad behavior and can trigger us to lash out at anyone who even hints we have sinned in a way we have unequivocally condemned.

This denial and blame shifting only goes so far, though. On the outside, we may even appear confident and at peace, but on the inside, we feel constant anxiety of becoming just like those we hate so much. Eventually, when we do something that we deem inexcusable, all the hatred we have aimed at others will reflect back at ourselves, and we will be crushed by our own harsh standards.

In Matthew 7:1-2, Jesus declares, "Judge not, that you be not judged. For with what judgment you judge, you will be judged; and with the measure you use, it will be measured back to you." (NKJV) This doesn't mean that we can't condemn sin in others, because condemning sin is the foundation of forgiveness. But if we condemn the sin yet withhold all hope of forgiveness and grace by judging them to the point that we won't even consider that they can change, then we will be judged in the same way. I have personally seen people who have become emotionally crippled, even suicidal, when they see within themselves even the faintest roots of the behaviors present in those who have hurt them. Because they can never accept that those who hurt them need grace as much as they do, they can also believe that they are beyond grace when they see those sins in themselves.

This shocking revelation can greatly increase their trauma as guilt locks them in their own minds and suffocates their growth. It reminds me of a man named Yehiel De-Nur, a Jewish Holocaust survivor who was asked to testify against Adolf Eichmann, one of the architects of the Nazi's "Final Solution to the Jewish question." When Yehiel entered the courtroom, he looked at Eichmann and broke down, sobbing and shouting uncontrollably, rendering him unable to testify. Many years later, Yehiel was interviewed by Mike Wallace on the CBS television news program 60 Minutes. He was asked if his response was due to hatred, trauma brought on by horrible memories, fear of the wickedness residing in Eichmann, or something else.

Incredibly, Yehiel stated that what drove him to weep the way he did was not the evil in Eichmann, but the humanity. He explained that he had envisioned Eichmann as being a demon who was easy to hate. But when Yehiel saw Eichmann that day in person, he was a man just like himself. The realization sent him reeling. "I was afraid about myself," Yehiel said. "I saw that I am capable to do this...exactly like he." It prompted Wallace to then say, "Eichmann is in all of us."

When you have suffered trauma at the hands of others, especially from someone close to you, the idea of choosing to see the humanity in that person and acknowledging the good that exists while condemning the evil can seem impossible. But refusing to do this deprives you of the true forgiveness that comes from Christ. It disables you from being able to see the common evil that exists in your own heart and recognizing that it is both condemned and forgiven at the cross. It also blinds you from seeing the wonderful hope in Jesus that there is no sinful behavior beyond His grace to help, no evil beyond His capacity to heal.

While the potential for untold evil exists in all of us, all potential for glory has been given to us through Christ.

Forgiveness and reconciliation

Another thing I had to learn was that forgiveness isn't the same as reconciliation. I found that it was actually easier to forgive members of the Taliban who fought against me, or even the abusive leaders I encountered in the Marines, than it was for me to forgive people in my everyday life who committed much smaller infractions. One reason for this was because I was never again going to see those who hurt me when I was in the military, but I actually had to deal with those who hurt me outside of the military.

As Christians, we are commanded to forgive, and it is done by ourselves in the presence of God, meaning we can forgive people without ever seeing them. However, to reconcile with someone means to repair and restore a relationship with them. That happens in the presence of the person who hurt us. Unlike forgiveness, believers in Christ are not explicitly commanded to reconcile, though it certainly is suggested in Romans 12:18-19, which says, "If it is possible, as much as depends on you, live peaceably with all men. Beloved, do not avenge yourselves, but rather give place to wrath; for it is written, 'Vengeance is Mine, I will repay,' says the Lord." (NKJV)

Notice that Paul tells us in this passage to live peaceably with others "as long as it depends on you." In other words, reconciliation isn't always up to you alone. Both parties have to be willing to make the relationship work. So, while the Bible elsewhere says to love your enemies, you don't have to be in a relationship with them. If someone you know is abusive toward you physically, mentally, or emotionally, and they are not showing any signs of true, genuine change, it is impossible for you to live peaceably with that person. Any attempt to do so will be sabotaged by their behavior, and they will continue to lash out at you and hurt you. This passage also affirms that we are to forgive everyone and "give place to wrath" by giving our anger to God and allowing Him to execute vengeance on our behalf. If you are afraid to forgive someone because you think you have to knowingly re-enter an abusive relationship to do so, that is not what God requires. What God does want is for you to be willing to reconcile with them if they actually start taking concrete steps to change and show authentic sorrow over what they have done.

Look at the life of Jesus. While He certainly did love all people, He didn't have relationships with everyone. One notable example was the Pharisees, who plotted with their fellow Jewish leaders to kill Him (Matthew 26). Jesus kept His distance from them, all the while loving them in any way that He could. But whenever someone began to change and desire a relationship with Jesus, He embraced that person with open arms. In John 3, we learn of a Pharisee named Nicodemus who visited Jesus secretly one night to discuss His teachings. Christ had a direct but loving dialogue with the Pharisee. A positive relationship was established, evidenced later when Nicodemus reminded his colleagues in the Sanhedrin that the law requires a person (such as Jesus) be heard before they judge him (John 7:50-51). Later still, Nicodemus' care for Jesus was shown by how he provided embalming spices for Christ's body after the crucifixion, and assisted Joseph of Arimathea in preparing the body for burial (John 19:39-42).

While the Bible teaches of loving and forgiving our enemies, we are also to be willing and constantly ready to serve them and meet their needs. In Romans 12:20-21, Paul continues, "Therefore 'If your enemy is hungry, feed him; If he is thirsty, give him a drink; For in so doing you will heap coals of fire on his head.' Do not be overcome by evil, but overcome evil with good." (NKJV) When Jesus did this for His enemies, it often happened as He met a physical need through a miracle or a blessing, but sometimes it also meant giving them a rebuke or a correction. Yet Jesus didn't actively seek vengeance on those who hurt Him. He didn't slander those who were against Him, nor did He call for an uprising against them. Instead, even as He was being killed by His enemies, Jesus prayed for them and asked the Father to forgive them (Luke 23:46).

In Proverbs 27:6, we read, "Faithful are the wounds of a friend, But the kisses of an enemy are deceitful." (NKJV) A friend shows someone his or her errors, but an enemy covers over errors and enables people in their destructive behavior. Jesus wasn't an enabler. He was willing to speak the truth, but He always did it in love. The rebukes Jesus gave were always out of care for the individual, not hatred. Some of us struggle because we hold in our anger and are unable or unwilling to express our pain to those who hurt us. Others have no problem expressing displeasure to others, but it is done in a selfish, judgmental, and damaging way. When we truly begin to forgive, we learn how to recognize the wrong that someone else is doing but meet it with loving correction instead of vindictive assaults.

This doesn't mean that you can't seek judicial punishment for those who have violated the law to abuse you. It is clear in Romans 13 that we are under the authority of the government, which is established by God to execute justice on our behalf. While I recognize as a Marine veteran that some of the actions we took in Afghanistan were wrong and beyond what should have been done (as I'll share shortly), our involvement there as a whole was sanctioned by our government to bring justice to the group that attacked our nation and our people. If you have been in armed combat, please understand that you weren't sinning or going against God's commands to love your enemies by fighting. You were functioning under the command of your government to bring justice to those seeking to harm others.

That said, we should not seek personal vengeance outside of the laws established by the government, nor are we to slander people in an attempt to expose the evil of what they've done to us. We are also not to physically try to get even with these people through force. Instead, we are to give God the right to judge them, so that we become free to love them, seek their betterment, and be willing to even enter into a relationship with them should they begin to genuinely change and show regret about their actions.

For most of us, this is a terrifying thought. It is far easier for me to assume that those who have hurt me are never going to change, letting me off the hook from ever having to relate to them again. But if I am going to be sincere in my forgiveness, then I should be praying for their betterment, wholeheartedly hoping that they do change. This introduces great fear in me, because I know that if they do start changing, then I am responsible to seek peace with them through reconciliation.

Since every situation is different, I encourage you to seek godly counsel, pray, and challenge yourself as you work through forgiving and potentially reconciling with those who have hurt you. The process of genuine forgiveness is a long one, and its duration and difficulty depends on how badly you have been wounded. Not only that, but it isn't a spontaneous thing. It'll take a concerted effort on your part to grow in your forgiveness and develop a genuine love for those who have hurt you. Even if reconciliation does happen, it is a fragile and arduous process because it takes time for true forgiveness to occur and for genuine change to happen in the person who caused your trauma. In almost every circumstance, there will be hurt on both sides and a need to forgive and change from both parties. Sometimes the relationship will be so damaged that it will never be exactly how it was, but peace and love can still exist. When you open yourself to this type of reconciliation birthed from forgiveness, it can be incredibly healing to you and those around you. However, you must diligently examine your heart, for it is very easy to deceive yourself into thinking you are open to reconciliation when you really aren't. You can place expectations on others that are unrealistic because, in actuality, you really don't want to reconcile with them and are unwilling to forgive. You convince yourself that the person is not repentant and not changing so you don't feel guilty about not being unwilling to reconcile.

One of the most prolific leaders in the civil rights movement, Dr. Martin Luther King Jr., helped me see this in great clarity through his powerful sermon entitled, "Loving Your Enemies." In it, he taught about the necessity to forgive and love, and the power of his words echo even louder when we recognize that he was talking about people who hated him so much they persecuted him and his family. As you read, know that no matter where you are in the process of forgiving those who have hurt you, the same message and power of the gospel that turned Dr. Martin Luther King Jr. into a man who would love his enemies, even at the cost of his own life, is available for you as well.

King preached:

"When you love [like God], you love all men, not because you like them, not because their ways appeal to you, not because they are worthwhile to you, but you love all men because God loves them. And you rise to the noble heights of loving the person who does the evil deed while hating the deed that the person does … I think this is what Jesus means when he says, 'Love your enemies.' And I'm so happy he didn't say, 'Like your enemies,' because it's kind of difficult to like some people. Like is sentimental. Like is an affectionate sort of thing. And you can't like anybody who's bombing your home and threatening your children. It's hard to like a senator who's spending all of his time in Washington standing against all of the legislation that will make for better relationships and that will make for brotherhood. It's difficult to like them."

"But Jesus says, 'Love them,' and love is greater than like. Love is understanding, redemptive, creative, goodwill for all men. And so Jesus was expressing something very creative when he said, 'Love your enemies. Bless them that curse you. Pray for them that despitefully use you.'"[iv]

Receiving forgiveness

Next, after learning how to forgive those who had hurt me, understanding how essential forgiveness was to receiving forgiveness myself, and becoming willing to reconcile even with those who were my enemies, I had to begin dealing with my own feelings of guilt. Once more, I had to not suppress these emotions, but face them with God and experience the wonders of true forgiveness.

For many of us dealing with PTSD, it will be our guilt that produces much of our trauma. It won't only exist in what we have seen, but we will be haunted by the thought that we were in some way responsible for what happened to us—and as our guilt grows, it will change into a far worse emotion: shame. Guilt is an emotion that is reactive to an action, while shame is a far deeper emotion that defames your very identity. When we feel guilty, we say, "I'm sorry. I made a mistake." But when we feel ashamed, we say, "I'm sorry. I *am* a mistake." Our burgeoning guilt and shame can permanently trap us in our trauma.

Most of the counsel I have received over the years has told me to excuse and ignore my guilt. I have been told that my actions in Afghanistan were not my fault because of the impossible situations I was in and that I needed to forgive myself, accepting that I don't have any culpability for what I did and what I saw. One incident in particular best illustrates this dilemma. After the Afghanis had harvested their poppy plants from which opium was derived for heroin or other pharmaceuticals, they placed the stacks of poppy stalks out in front of their houses to later use for firewood. Whenever we walked by their homes, we ignored these stacks, knowing how they were going to be used. The Taliban, however, figured this out, and they started placing IEDs under the piles to set off when we walked by. A couple of my buddies were blown up by these hidden IEDs.

In response, we began searching the poppy stalks for the explosives—and we found an IED kit, complete with the copper wires, battery, and everything that was needed, in front of a family's house. We went in and interrogated the man in front of his wife and children, roughing him up a bit in the process. He vehemently insisted he knew nothing about the kit, but we didn't believe him.

We took him to our base to be detained, separating him from his family, and then lit his fields and his home on fire while his wife and children stood to the side and watched in horror.

The next day, one of our informants, an individual in the city that we knew was loyal to us, met with my company. He went into his backyard and returned with an IED kit. It was exactly like the one we had found in front of the home we destroyed.

"What's going on?" one of my fellow Marines asked. "Where did you get that?"

"The Taliban has identified all of the people and families who are loyal to you, and they have planted these in front of their homes, beneath the poppy stalks, so that you'll detain them.

I gasped. *We just ruined that guy's life,* I thought. *We burned down his house, we burned down his field, he doesn't have any money, we don't know what happened to his wife and kids, and now this guy is detained at our base.* He was released, but, to my knowledge, he wasn't compensated in any way for his losses.

I was involved with other incidents as bad as, or worse than, that one. I didn't feel guilty about it for quite a while. I knew I should've. I had been involved in something that turned out wrong. If the same thing had been done to someone in the United States, there would've been serious consequences—but because we did it over there, it was just swept under the rug and excused.

For the longest time, I'd think back to what happened and feel justified in my actions. *It was war,* I reasoned. *We didn't have a choice.* I pushed it aside. But that only amplified my pride, causing me to feel like I never had to admit I was wrong or sorry about anything. It made me more self-centered and more justified in all the wrong things that I did. It wasn't until well after that incident and others I experienced as a Marine in Afghanistan that I first felt sad, then angry. As that anger led me to seek God, I began to realize that I *should* feel guilty. So, I started asking for forgiveness from God even though I didn't actually feel guilty.

That process slowly allowed me to genuinely *be* guilty about those actions and receive forgiveness for them at the same time. I realized, for example, that I didn't order the man's house to be burned. The patrol leader did, but I didn't do anything about it, either. Therefore, I felt guilty about not speaking up or trying to stop it.

When we tell ourselves that the things in our past aren't our fault, the coping mechanism of increased self-importance can easily extend beyond our past, and we'll be tempted to implement this strategy every time we experience feelings of guilt. As bad as our guilt can be, it *is* our guilt that moves us to admit wrong and seek to change. Without guilt, we aren't able to apologize for incorrect actions or adjust our behavior, but we can instead become masters at shifting blame to other people or to the past itself.

There are also those who will never be able to successfully forgive themselves. They will try over and over again to do so, but those old familiar feelings of guilt and shame will rise up until they are unable to hold back those feelings. When that happens, they become consumed by self-condemnation and fear. They lose control over their emotions, and the solution that was supposed to make them better only ends up making them feel worse.

Psalm 32:1-5 declares, "Blessed is he whose transgression is forgiven, Whose sin is covered. Blessed is the man to whom the Lord does not impute iniquity, And in whose spirit there is no deceit. When I kept silent, my bones grew old Through my groaning all the day long. For day and night Your hand was heavy upon me; My vitality was turned into the drought of summer. I acknowledged my sin to You, And my iniquity I have not hidden. I said, 'I will confess my transgressions to the Lord,' And You forgave the iniquity of my sin." (NKJV)

As Christians, we need to realize that the emotion of guilt was given to us by God to help us understand our guilt before Him. Only God has the right to judge us; therefore, only He has the authority to forgive us for what we have done. When we understand this, we can begin to bring our guilt before God and ask Him to help us understand our guilt and receive His forgiveness. In King David's prayer from Psalm 32, he reveals that when he tried to forgive himself, he had no peace, but instead felt a constant burden on his soul. It dried up his emotional vitality and emptied him of passion. However, when he brought his guilt before God, he found the peace that comes from accepting God's forgiveness.

When we pray, we should express our feelings of guilt and shame to God, asking Him to reveal the truth of our emotions. Doing this over time, combined with the help of counseling, will help you see how much fault you actually carry from what happened to you. We tend to think in black and white, believing that something either was or wasn't completely our fault. What we discover, though, is that bringing our guilt to God is more complicated than that. Most of the time, there will be shared guilt between ourselves and others. We will see that some of what happened was our fault, but other parts of it were really out of our hands. Even for those who conclude that what happened to them was in no way their fault, they may recognize how some of their behavior in response to what happened was their fault, and they will need forgiveness for those actions. This might be potentially stumbling or difficult to understand for those who have been through abusive childhoods, but it's important to know that, while it is possible that everything that happened to them in their childhood was not their fault or caused by them, that doesn't totally excuse the behaviors.

As we seek the Lord in prayer, we will also find that a lot of our feelings of guilt weren't actually because we sinned against God, but against our own ideas of right and wrong. It would be great if we could perfectly discern right and wrong as God does, but the truth is we gradually develop our own interpretations of right and wrong through what was told to us by our families, our culture, our friends, and our own thinking. This places us in a situation where we can never receive real peace through forgiveness. Much of what we feel guilty about is not wrong at all in the eyes of God. Rather, He is the only One who can rightly determine our guilt and truly forgive us because He is the only One who actually paid the price for what we have done through giving His own life for ours. If we sin against anything else, whether it is our own views of right and wrong or against someone else whose opinion we have elevated above God's, we won't find peace unless we fully "pay" for what we have done—and we can never pay enough to cover that.

This doesn't mean that we shouldn't make amends with those we have legitimately wronged. After David committed adultery with a married woman, Bathsheba, and murdered her husband, Uriah, he wrote, "Against You, You only, have I sinned," (Psalm 51:4, NKJV), meaning that while he clearly sinned against other people, he understood that God was the ultimate offended party for his sin, and therefore, the ultimate judge from whom he needed forgiveness. This perspective did not make David cold and calloused toward those he had hurt. It made him more diligent and selfless in his desire to make things right with them.

If we try to make amends solely to gain the forgiveness of someone else, we are motivated by a selfish desire to assuage our guilt. Some of us only seek to make things right with someone else when our efforts are being rewarded and noticed. We'll become impatient and angry if the person is slow or hesitant to forgive, and usually just give up trying altogether. Others will incarcerate themselves in a prison of their own guilt while they endlessly attempt to receive forgiveness from someone who obviously doesn't possess the desire or ability to give them the forgiveness they need.

Making others the source of our forgiveness can cause so much guilt and shame, we can never move forward. That's why we need to place God in His right place in our hearts, seeing that He alone is the judge of all the earth and, at the end of the day, only His opinion of us matters. As we do this, it will expose wrongs that we didn't even realize we had done because God's standards are far higher and different than anyone else's. Yet we won't be afraid to confront our guilt because we will confidently, even joyously, pray like David did in Psalm 139:23-24 when he proclaimed, "Search me, O God, and know my heart; Try me, and know my anxieties; And see if there is any wicked way in me, And lead me in the way everlasting." (NKJV).

This is especially important to understand for those of us who battle with a feeling of distance between us and God because of our mistakes. This was most pronounced in my life through my struggle with pornography. I first saw pornography when I was quite young, and guilt over my sexual sin was the reason why I became an atheist when I was 13 years old. I didn't want God's standards in my life because I felt terrible that I wasn't keeping them. I remained an atheist for three years before giving my life back to God when I was 16. Yet I still struggled with the sexual sin of viewing pornography—and I found that every time I failed, I felt like I wasn't a Christian. It was as though I wasn't really saved. I figured God was becoming frustrated or disappointed with me to the point that I had no place with Him. After viewing pornography, I wouldn't even talk to God for a week or so because I was too ashamed. But, after a week of trying to do good, Christian acts and going to church, I'd feel comfortable enough to talk to Him again. Until I looked at porn. Then I'd start the same, tired cycle.

I eventually came to a point where I was so ashamed about what I was doing that I actually prayed that God would leave me. I wanted Him to literally take His Holy Spirit away from me because I felt so guilty. I looked back to my time as an atheist and thought, *I was pretty unhappy then, but at least I was happier than I am now.* When I said that prayer, God brought to mind Romans 5:20. "Where sin abounded, grace abounded much more." (NKJV) That told me that I couldn't "out sin" God's grace. I heard the Lord tell my spirit, "I am not going to give up on you. I'm not just going to cast you aside. I am with you. I am for you."

That was such an amazing moment. Later, I read Hosea 11, an Old Testament chapter about God's continuing love for His people, the Israelites. Hosea tells the story of a husband who is constantly being cheated on by his wife, and the whole message of the book is that even though God sees our sin as personally violating to Him as being cheated on by an unfaithful spouse would be, His love is still so much deeper and greater than our sin.

Speaking of the 10 northern tribes of Israel as Ephraim, God said in Hosea 11:3-4, "I taught Ephraim to walk, Taking them by their arms; But they did not know that I healed them. I drew them with gentle cords, With bands of love, And I was to them as those who take the yoke from their neck. I stooped and fed them." (NKJV) I then understood that God was not an angry, disappointed Father looking down on me from heaven in frustration every time I sinned sexually. Instead, He was a patient Father teaching me to walk in His righteousness. My sin didn't need to separate me from God. It drew Him to me so that He could lift me up, and I could try again to walk better the next time.

The place that we need to go for peace when our guilt and shame seek to pull us away from God is the cross. Remember Romans 5:8-9. It declares, "But God demonstrates His own love toward us, in that while we were still sinners, Christ died for us. Much more then, having now been justified by His blood, we shall be saved from wrath through Him." (NKJV)

In the presence of God, we recognize that while we are far more guilty than we believed, we are also completely forgiven and far more loved than we could ever hope—and our delight will then be to please the Lord, who is so pleased with us. Colossians 1:20-22 tells us how the Father, through Christ, was able to "reconcile all things to Himself, by Him, whether things on earth or things in heaven, having made peace through the blood of His cross. And you, who once were alienated and enemies in your mind by wicked works, yet now He has reconciled in the body of His flesh through death, to present you holy, and blameless, and above reproach in His sight." (NKJV)

We are reconciled to God in Christ, and we need to accept and receive what God says about us. True faith isn't believing something because we feel it. True faith is accepting something even when all of our emotions are communicating something completely different. We need to believe simply because God says it is so and we trust Him. It may be true that we have failed in various areas, but it is also true that Jesus Christ came to redeem sinners, not the righteous. As we consider the cross, we should see that no matter how horrific our actions, or the hurts committed against us, Jesus paid the price. It may sound humble to say, "I know God forgives me, but I can't forgive myself," yet such a statement is actually incredibly arrogant. The reality is we do not have the authority to judge or forgive ourselves. Only God has that right— and because of what He has done for us, in spite of what we have done, He calls us holy and blameless. As Paul reminds us in 1 Corinthians 4:3-4, "But with me it is a very small thing that I should be judged by you or by a human court. In fact, I do not even judge myself. For I know of nothing against myself, yet I am not justified by this; but He who judges me is the Lord." (NKJV)

Because of our sins, God had righteous wrath toward us. But because of Jesus, that wrath has been taken away and we are now forgiven and accepted by God. Since God has accepted you and forgiven you, who are you to argue with your Creator? When the reality of your guilt and the truth of God's forgiveness for you meet, shame is swept away, and real healing can begin.

If Jesus loved you enough to die for you at your worst, you can believe, in spite of your emotions, that His love and forgiveness remain regardless of what you have done or what has been done to you. He died so that you might have life, meaning that your life, the one you had so devalued in your guilt and shame, has infinite value in God through Christ's sacrifice. The way you determine the value of something is by seeing what someone is willing to pay for it. Do you realize that when God evaluated the cost of your life, He was willing to purchase it with His own blood? What in all of creation is more valuable than the blood of Jesus?

Your life has value. You can live knowing that He has a plan and a purpose for your life, and that there is hope for you that you can't even begin to fully understand.

God bought you with a price. So you must honor God with your body.
1 Corinthians 6:20, NLT

Chapter 7
Identifying with Our Trauma

A woman named Thordis Elva was raped as a teenager by her then-boyfriend, Tom. In a very emotional TED Talk, both her and Tom shared their own journeys of healing, forgiveness, and reconciliation. During the presentation, Thordis said this about negative labels:

"Given the nature of our story, I know the words that inevitably accompany it—victim, rapist—and labels are a way to organize concepts, but they can also be dehumanizing in their connotations. Once someone's been deemed a victim, it's that much easier to file them away as someone damaged, dishonored, less than. And, likewise, once someone has been branded a rapist, it's that much easier to call him a monster, inhuman. But how will we understand what it is in human societies that produces violence if we refuse to recognize the humanity of those who commit it? And how can we empower survivors if we're making them feel less than? How can we discuss solutions to one of the biggest threats to the lives of women and children around the world if the very words we use are part of the problem?"[v]

If we choose to identify with our trauma and embrace an identity about ourselves based on a label—whether we are a victim or a perpetrator, or if we have a psychological disorder or some other mental diagnosis—we will lose our very humanity, individuality, and ability to heal, relate to others, and change. Likewise, if we apply these labels to others, we will lose our ability to treat our fellow humans as individuals, empathize with their pain, and truly help them.

Our modern culture has witnessed a huge growth in our understanding of the human psyche and how we think and operate in our daily lives. This has allowed us to discover that we are not all the same. Some of us have mental disorders that we were either born with or that were developed through trauma, and these disorders play a significant role in how we function. However, if we start to only see ourselves through the label of those disorders, it can be really damaging.

Why? These disorders include broad categories of struggles and issues, yet anyone can casually go online, look up these disorders, and even chat with a mental health "expert" who knows nothing about them to receive a recommendation or diagnosis that may be inaccurate or incomplete. My story proves how such increasingly common conditions as PTSD and depression can be so complicated and different for one person than they are for others. We have to see ourselves as individuals, not labels.

In addition, we have to learn to accept the truth about ourselves from God so that we don't begin to identify ourselves by our trauma or its label. We cannot afford for the bad things that happened to us in the past to morph from being just unfortunate events to becoming the source of our identity—for when we do, we will see ourselves as being damaged victims or monsters trapped in our past. It's that type of polarized thinking that can permanently prevent us from ever experiencing the healing God has for us.

My trauma doesn't define me. What happened to me in the military was a very important part of my life, but it isn't solely responsible for the man I am now. The issues I struggle with today were intensified by my negative experiences, but they weren't created by my two deployments. I battled with anger, pride, fear, insecurity, shame, depression, and much more well before I went to Afghanistan. When we identify with our trauma, we can believe the false idea that, "If only that didn't happen to me, I wouldn't have any of my issues," or, "The reason why I act the way I do is because of what happened to me, and if I can just heal from my past, I won't struggle anymore." We can even come to assume that others around us don't have any real or valid issues in their lives because they aren't damaged like we are, causing us to feel that we are nothing more than dead weight in our relationships.

Beyond that, as Thordis pointed out earlier, when someone is labeled, it is easy to see them as less than human. It is tragic, but those loaded mental labels can make us look at others as if they are from another planet. They can also make us feel like we can't relate to them at all, so we don't even try and might even become afraid of them. Those of us who have received or accepted those negative labels can see ourselves as being an "other," like we don't really belong anywhere and are incapable of changing.

The Bible teaches that our issues didn't begin with a traumatic event or a disorder, but much earlier. Psalm 51:5 says, "Behold, I was brought forth in iniquity, And in sin my mother conceived me." (NKJV)

David wrote this after having the affair with Bathsheba and murdering her husband (2 Samuel 11). He could have easily identified with his past actions and blamed his upbringing on being overshadowed by his older brothers, or his trauma on being introduced to war at such a young age, or his pain from being hunted like an animal for years by King Saul. But David didn't do any of this. He acknowledged that his issues stemmed from the original sin that he possessed when he was born. While his experiences did amplify his later issues, they didn't create them. Even without his trauma, he would've still had character defects caused by sin that, left unchecked, would create all sorts of problems in his life.

An understanding of sin is the great leveler for the Christian. All of us were brought forth in iniquity, which in the Hebrew refers to an inherent bentness or a natural propensity toward wrong. We all are born with this and, therefore, we will all struggle with sinful behavior. Some of our behavior is more outwardly destructive than others, but all of it is sin before God, and all of it has to be judged and forgiven by Him.

Beyond that, the scariest thing I have discovered as I've counseled others is that trauma and disorders are nothing more than exaggerated versions of what everyone deals with on a regular basis. When I speak to someone who has PTSD, an anxiety disorder, or depression, while their behavior may be far more extreme than other people, the emotional roots of their problems aren't too different from everyone else's. Their behavior is harder to control, but the roots are the same. I am not saying that your past has no bearing on your present. It definitely does. Examining and learning from our past can provide a good understanding of many of our issues and why we act the way we do. But that doesn't mean that our issues were created solely by our past trauma and disorders.

The trauma of my past magnified my issues, so healing and learning to cope with them is vital to my growth in Christ, but it isn't the end of my growth, and it certainly isn't my only problem. God wants to heal us and help us grow, but our main issue is our separation from Him caused by our sin. When we understand that our main problem is our separation from God, then we will pursue Him, not merely for healing, but because He is worthy—and we understand our great need is for Him alone, not for what He can give to us.

Creating trauma

Unfortunately, we also have to be aware of the possibility of exaggerating and even manufacturing trauma in our minds. I say this with a lot of care because I do not want anyone to think that I am in some way denying the pain they have gone through or suggesting they are faking their symptoms. However, it is true that there is a very real danger of our minds and our hearts deceiving us to convince us of things that aren't necessarily true. As Jeremiah 17:9 states, "The heart is deceitful above all things, And desperately wicked; Who can know it?" (NKJV)

This is an especially dangerous possibility in our overly sensitive culture that tends to casually throw out diagnoses. It is possible, for a number of reasons, that someone can begin to believe that their past is far more traumatic than it really was, and in turn, actually manifest the symptoms of PTSD. One way this can happen is when a person is misdiagnosed with PTSD by someone else. They can so strongly believe that they have PTSD, they will make the symptoms real in their own mind. The same thing can occur when a doctor tells someone they have a particular illness. Heard from a trusted source, they can start to believe the diagnosis even if it isn't accurate. Our minds can then fabricate physical symptoms psychosomatically, caused or aggravated by our own mental conflict, fear, or belief.

It is possible for someone to have a hypochondriac mentality, becoming so afraid they are sick that they actually make themselves ill. Others can so subconsciously want to be sick they make themselves that way. This person can hear or read about symptoms of some sort of illness and mentally create these symptoms in themselves without even knowing it. This can also be true with mental disorders. Someone who doesn't actually have an anxiety-based disorder can become so afraid or convinced they do have it that their mind makes it real.

There are a myriad of reasons why someone would want to exaggerate or even manufacture trauma. One of the primary reasons comes from a desire or need to have a status as a victim. In the past, to be from a broken background was a shameful thing in our society. People who had suffered were made to feel less than others because of what they had been through. Our culture has tried to correct that by giving more attention, respect, and understanding to those who have had traumatic pasts. That's not a bad thing. But this has made some people covet a traumatic past in order to get more attention, validation, and sometimes even an excuse to act out in negative ways without consequences or having to listen to correction. I've even seen people outright fake symptoms of PTSD to gain and maintain a victim status.

Another common reason people exaggerate or manufacture trauma is to validate an extreme emotion. The mind is a fragile thing, and sometimes there can be a different mental disorder or breakdown from excessive stress or grief that can cause someone to have an overly emotional response to something that has happened to them. Because it is so difficult to sort through emotions during a time like this, their mind will naturally overemphasize the past in order to validate their extreme emotion. Finally, it is also possible for someone to do this as a result of using bitterness and anger to cover over past pain. So, when they try to shield themselves from their hurt, they increasingly magnify the past to rationalize their growing indignation at the person who wounded them. They can do this until their version of the past is so exaggerated that it hardly resembles the truth at all.

Whatever the cause of abnormally powerful emotions, mental attempts to justify them can, in turn, create PTSD symptoms. However, if we address these issues like normal PTSD, we can completely miss the real cause of the problem—which is not what we've actually been through, but the way our mind has processed it. It's kind of like someone who has a physical illness that causes them to be more fragile so that even a small thing causes severe bruising or a fractured bone. While the injury needs to be addressed, the more pressing matter is the cause of the fragility.

It is important to validate and help someone with their trauma, but it is even more important to find out why they have been so traumatized by something that shouldn't have had as extreme an impact on them as it did. Why did what happened, and the person's reaction and ability to properly process it, fail to match up? Something else is causing their extreme reaction, and if it isn't addressed, they will be far more vulnerable to being traumatized again, and that will undermine their healing process. It can also cause unfair amounts of blame to be leveled against others in their lives. It's vital for us to be aware of the very real possibility of our own hearts being deceived. This will take a very high level of bravery and brutal self-evaluation, but we must challenge ourselves to discover whether the primary problem was our experience or how we processed it.

It can also be helpful to go through this process with a counselor, but we have to be bold because if we have exaggerated or fabricated our trauma, it will be painful, difficult, and even embarrassing to let go of our version of the events in the presence of another person. But remember, if the problem was how we processed our experience, that doesn't invalidate it or mean that the symptoms will go away. We'll still need to work through those memories, and perhaps have to reevaluate and change our therapy approach, to help us best deal with the root problem of our trauma. I remember a conversation I had with a counselor who was working with a woman that had come out of a failed marriage. The woman was at a point in her therapy where she believed the marriage had been physically abusive. Problem was, I knew for a fact that wasn't the case. I asked the counselor, "Do you actually know that this guy was abusive? Do you really know that this was the actual version of the events?"

"Well, you know," he said, "we all have our own version of events, and it's just important for me to validate where she's at, because she's had so little validation in her life."

I was taken aback and pressed him on the issue. "But don't you think that's a little damaging, to take someone who hasn't actually been through an abusive marriage and validate them into thinking that they have been in one?"

"No," he replied adamantly. "She just hasn't had any validation in her life, and this is what she needs."

I realized the counselor's approach was not making the woman better. It was making her worse. To this day, she is completely convinced that she was in an abusive marriage. Was it dysfunctional? Yes. Was its failure in and of itself traumatic? Absolutely. But the level of trauma that she experienced was simply not congruent with what really happened.

Finally, friends and family members could be helpful as well, but only if they have proven to be gentle and honest with you, even when it hurts. It is easy for friends and family to likewise falsely validate you and your trauma because of their love for you, but that will only sink you deeper into your version of the events instead of helping you see the truth. If at all possible, talk to an unbiased source who was present during the time of your trauma to help you sort through all of this.

Dealing with our dual nature

Knowing the truth about our trauma is also key when it comes to our guilt and how we deal with others in the face of that trauma. Dorothy L. Sayers was a famous Christian author who once said, in the aftermath of World War II, that it was the biblical view of the inherent sinful nature of man that was a great strength for her in understanding the evil that exists in ourselves and others. She believed that those who held the position that mankind was basically good and could be civilized through mere human effort were decimated when confronted with the atrocities done during the war. Their hope and confidence were gone, and they had no ability to deal with the evil they saw in themselves or others because they lacked an appropriate understanding of human nature.

But Sayers wrote, "Now for the Christian, this is not so. He is as deeply shocked and grieved as anyone else, but he is not astonished. He has been accustomed to the idea that there is a deep interior dislocation in the very center of human personality. The delusion of the mechanical perfectibility of mankind through a combined process of scientific knowledge and unconscious evolution has been responsible for a great deal of heartbreak. It is, at bottom, far more pessimistic than Christian pessimism because, if science and progress break down, there is nothing to fall back upon. Humanism is self-contained—it provides for man no resources outside himself. The Christian dogma of the double nature of man—which asserts that man is disintegrated and necessarily imperfect in himself and all his works, yet closely related by a real unity of substance with an eternal perfection within and beyond them—makes the present parlous state of human society seem less hopeless and less irrational."[vi]

Essentially, Sayers states that we like to see ourselves as being relatively good people with the ability to save ourselves. This belief makes us feel better, but it ultimately sets us up for truly traumatic disillusionments. PTSD, for many people, is triggered by a type of identity crisis. For some, this happens because they always saw themselves as good, decent people, but then they perform actions they see as terrible and inexcusable. When we see ourselves as monsters, and we can't reconcile that with the good people we thought we were, we can have a mental breakdown caused by guilt. For others, this can happen when they have a relationship with someone that they saw as good and loving. Over time and through repeated damaging actions performed by the other person, we realize that the relationship wasn't what we thought. We discover we were believing a false reality and that the relationship was anything but a fairy tale. We can't reconcile the years we thought were so beautiful with the existing dysfunction.

However, if we accept the truth about ourselves and others that the Bible reveals, we realize that without God, we are all desperately wicked and capable of every kind of evil. It's not that we will necessarily do evil, but evil lies within us. In our pride, we assume we are good, so when the reality of our inner evil rears its ugly head, we can be crushed under the weight of guilt and shame. It's only when we are able to humble ourselves and see the weight of our own sin that we can also see with greater clarity the wonderful truth of God's love for us in spite of our sin. As Paul declares in 1 Timothy 1:15-16, "This is a faithful saying and worthy of all acceptance, that Christ Jesus came into the world to save sinners, of whom I am chief. However, for this reason I obtained mercy, that in me first Jesus Christ might show all longsuffering, as a pattern to those who are going to believe on Him for everlasting life." (NKJV)

In this passage, as Paul dealt with his past guilt from persecuting Christians and his current guilt from the sins he still struggled against, he didn't make excuses, but instead declared himself the "chief" of sinners. But he didn't say that out of self-pity or despair, but triumphantly as he peered through the extreme darkness of his sin and saw how much brighter the light of Christ's love and forgiveness was for him. Paul saw his old identity grounded in his past failures washed away by the blood of Christ, finding his new identity in the faithfulness of God alone.

We need to do the same. All of us have negative self-identities built, brick by brick, by the things we have done and been through. The terrible thing about these built identities is that we become walled in by them, unable to change or escape them. If someone kills one person, he becomes a murderer. It doesn't matter if he never kills anyone ever again. He remains a murderer because of what he did. In the same way, if someone is abused just once, they become a victim, even if they spend the rest of their lives away from abuse. Because of what happened to them in the past, that identity sticks with them, and it can't be washed away by time or effort. Most of us spend our lives trying to build a better identity than the one we have already made for ourselves. We may even run from place to place trying to escape our past, only to realize that it is impossible to run from ourselves.

But the beauty of Jesus is that while we all have identities as sinners, He came to give us new identities that are received through faith in Him. Christ didn't just bear our sin. He literally became sin for us. Even though Jesus had built for Himself a perfect identity through His flawless obedience to the law all of His life, He chose to lay that aside and become our sin for us (2 Corinthians 5:21). By taking our identity as sinners upon Himself, Jesus made it so we could receive His identity as righteous. This doesn't occur through any actions we can perform or experiences we can go through, but solely through faith in Jesus and what He has done for us. That faith allows us to finally rise above our negative self-identities of seeing ourselves as damaged, victims, murderers, adulterers, and so on, and identify ourselves as holy and blameless children of God.

It is purely by faith that we accept our identity as His child because all of the evidence can seem to be to the contrary. But if we can grow in our faith and receive more and more the truth of who we are through the grace of God, we can understand, as Sayers did, that we have a dual nature. We are desperately wicked, but with God living in us and through us, we are righteous and capable of every good. We'll no longer be proud, ignorant people unconcerned by the damage we have done to others. We won't be hard, calloused people who act like we aren't bothered by our pain. We will be grieved by our past trauma and actions, but we will not be crushed or dismayed without hope for change or redemption for our past. We will be able to accept forgiveness for our sins and hope, through the work of Christ in us, that every scar we have will be healed, redeemed, and used by Him as we are gradually changed into His very image and likeness for His glory. This isn't so we can *gain* a better identity, but because we have already *received* one by grace through faith in God.

The full realization of this truth in my life was a slow learning process. It first began back when I asked God to take His Holy Spirit from me and recalled Romans 5:20, then later as I read through Hosea. Intellectually, I knew that I was saved by grace through faith and had received a new identity in Christ, but acceptance of that truth came subtly over the years. As His grace gradually became reality for me, it certainly contributed to my ongoing healing from my past traumas. The level of healing that we attain is proportionate to our acceptance of His truth about grace.

This also helps us with our trust issues. Those of us who have been through severe trauma develop trust issues because we may have been confronted by the horrible evil of others. When that happens, it can be nearly impossible to fully trust people ever again. When we see the true evil of humanity in the darkness of war, through physical, mental, or sexual abuse, or from something else that is terrible, we can't simply dismiss it. Most people have the ability to trust because they live in an illusion that people are basically good. The rest of us have been confronted with the truth that humanity is capable of horrendous things, and when we see just how awful this is, we can wall ourselves off, treating everything and everyone else as a threat.

However, it is this same truth about the dual nature of man that gives us the ability to open ourselves to others as we have faith in God. That doesn't mean that we are to be naive and totally vulnerable with everyone. Instead, we allow ourselves to cautiously develop relationships with others under the umbrella of hope given to us by our God. Knowing that He is our protector and our defender, we can sincerely believe, just as Paul did, that if God can work in our lives, He can do the same work in anyone. Paul was once a bigoted persecutor of Christians, but God transformed him into one of the most loving and peaceful individuals to ever walk the earth. This gave Paul the confidence to reach out to extremely violent people, even though it ultimately cost him his life. He believed in God's power and ability to redeem the vile heart of man. He trusted so supremely in the love of God and in the protection of his Father that he knew that there was nothing that could be taken away from him on earth that would ever measure up to what he was gaining in Christ.

We must be led by this same belief and allow it to give us hope to open up to others and trust in the power of God in their lives as well as our own. We should never knowingly enter into abusive relationships or reconcile with abusive people. But we can enter into relationships with others without constantly reacting to the fears of our past and projecting that anxiety and pain onto our current relationships. We do not have to treat people who haven't hurt us as if they will abuse or abandon us. This belief will also help us to forgive others, pray for their salvation and change, and even carefully reach out to those who have hurt us if we see change in them. It gives us hope and peace in our relationships as we learn to trust more in God's protection of our hearts and His divine work in others.

For He made Him who knew no sin to be sin for us,
that we might become the righteousness of God in Him.
2 Corinthians 5:21, NKJV

Chapter 8
Growing in Peace

One of the main symptoms of Post-Traumatic Stress Disorder is paralyzing anxiety. There are many reasons people have an unhealthy amount of stress, but some of the most common causes are from having our mental and emotional strain pushed to their limits in the midst of trauma and then being unable to recalibrate our fear levels to function in everyday life. Unhealthy stress can also come from our feelings of helplessness and regret about our past that make us feel out of control and powerless to do anything about our current and future problems.

Andrew Solomon is an author and speaker who has written a lot about depression. In one of his TED Talks about depression, he described a time in his life when he struggled with anxiety:

"Then the anxiety set in. If you told me that I'd have to be depressed for the next month, I would say, "As long as I know it'll be over in November, I can do it." But if you said to me, "You have to have acute anxiety for the next month," I would rather slit my wrist than go through it. It was the feeling all the time, like if you're walking and you slip or trip and the ground is rushing up at you, but instead of lasting half a second the way that does, it lasted for six months. It's a sensation of being afraid all the time but not even knowing what it is that you're afraid of. It was at that point that I began to think that it was just too painful to be alive, and that the only reason not to kill oneself was so as not to hurt other people."[vii]

Feeling like this can be overwhelming and can even push someone to the point of being suicidal just to make the feeling stop. It can also drive someone to substance abuse as they desperately try to turn off their powerful emotions. Experiencing that level of anxiety day in and day out is the real hell of PTSD—but through God, we can learn to grow in peace.

Philippians 4:6-7 declares, "Be anxious for nothing, but in everything by prayer and supplication, with thanksgiving, let your requests be made known to God; and the peace of God, which surpasses all understanding, will guard your hearts and minds through Christ Jesus." (NKJV) This passage does not claim that dealing with anxiety is easy, as some Christians have made it out to say. What it does do is encourage us to constantly bring our fears and feelings of helplessness before God and pray to see, by faith, the truth that when we feel we aren't in control, He is. The Bible assures us that God always has a purpose for everything that is happening to us. Job, an Old Testament character who experienced untold levels of stress and trauma, said of the Lord, "I know that You can do everything, And that no purpose of Yours can be withheld from You." (Job 42:2, NKJV)

Paralyzing anxiety sets in only when we think we are in control and are ultimately responsible for what has happened and what will happen. This can be a particularly challenging problem to address for most of us, especially combat vets, because it was our stress and our training that helped keep us safe. When we were in a consistently chaotic and dangerous environment, we had to be constantly on alert. One lapse into complacency could cost us our lives. In a combat situation, it was a good thing to wake up at the slightest sound, overanalyze every possible threat, and always be ready for the next fight. However, when we got back home, that level of vigilance was no longer a good thing and could begin to destroy us. Why? Being overly vigilant in a peacetime environment is draining to the psyche. It causes us to be mentally exhausted, sleepless, paranoid, jumpy, stressed out, and overreactive to normal things. Relevant retraining to enable us to reacclimate to a non-combat life is needed so we can recalibrate our caution to suit the current environment. If we're overly stressed when it isn't warranted for the situation, we need to learn how to turn our caution down. If we're under-stressed when the situation warrants more caution, we need to know how to turn it up.

This isn't easy. Learning how to control the heightened caution that protected us in the military is difficult. It begins by analyzing the situation and our reactions and asking, "Is this an appropriate amount of stress to have over my current situation?" "Was that an appropriate *reaction* to what was happening?" "What am I afraid of in this situation?" "Is this a rational thing to be worried about?" If we never evaluate our stress level, we will always react toward things based on what we are used to doing—and for those of us who have been through severe trauma, that reaction is usually not positive or healthy.

This is not something we do every now and then, but it has to become a brand-new discipline we incorporate daily in our lives. It requires a lot of personal meditation, evaluation, and diligence, thinking through and being sensitive to our reactions. It necessitates talking about our reactions with those we trust enough to help us in the recovery process. But the more we do this, the easier and more helpful it will be.

As hard as this is for military veterans, it can be more difficult for police officers, firefighters, medical professionals, and those who have suffered trauma in their own homes. For me and my fellow Marines, as bad as our deployments were, we did leave our combat zone and come home. We left our environment of trauma, and while it takes time and effort to reacclimate, our home wasn't where we were traumatized. Everyone else has to learn how to avoid and cope with the trauma triggers that exist all around them.

When we get triggered by something from our past and start feeling anxious about it, we need to immediately bring those fears to God in prayer. We must be brutally honest and descriptive about our fears, asking God for the strength to accept that we can't change what happened or control what will happen. As we do this, God will help us grow in our faith toward Him and in our ability to cope with our fears. Interestingly, my most challenging experiences with trauma triggers and the fears they can cause have had nothing to do with my time in Afghanistan. As a marriage counselor and associate pastor, I sadly see marriages fail all the time. Because of that, I'd come home after a day at the church and begin noticing things in my marriage that reminded me of the same issues that I'd seen with the couples I'd counseled. It would kind of freak me out, causing me to become overly controlling with my wife, Emma, and try to fix problems that weren't even there. That manipulative response to my trauma triggers from work started to wreck my own marriage as we had disagreements or outright arguments over these perceived issues. I had to learn to discipline myself to pray, bring those issues and fears before God, and ask Him for the power to be present and not project what I'd seen in the counseling office onto her, myself, or our marriage. I still work at not being overly sensitive in our marriage but instead able to properly analyze situations without assuming the worst.

In addition, we need to see the reality of God's authority and love in our lives in order to grow in peace. For some of us, we can't receive His peace because we don't trust God. We have seen Him "fail" us too many times and now feel solely responsible for keeping our lives intact. Through confronting our animosity toward God and growing in our faith that He is not only all powerful but also all loving, our peace will increase right along with our faith.

Notable biblical personalities struggled greatly with their animosity toward the Lord. At one point, Jeremiah flat out accused God of deceiving him (Jeremiah 20:7) because he thought he was going to deliver the people of Israel through his prophetic ministry to them. Yet the more he preached, the more people hated him. Jeremiah poured out his frustration to God. "The word of the Lord was made to me A reproach and a derision daily. Then I said, 'I will not make mention of Him, Nor speak anymore in His name.' But His word was in my heart like a burning fire Shut up in my bones; I was weary of holding it back, And I could not." (Jeremiah 20:8-9, NKJV) The more Jeremiah realized how out of control of the situation he was, the more stressed out he became, and he grew angry at God. It wasn't until much later on in his ministry that Jeremiah was able to declare his hope in the Lord and his belief that His love never failed (Lamentations 3:21-22). Jeremiah realized that while he was mad at the Lord for allowing the situation, he was also able to accept God's peace and understand that He was ultimately in control of it all.

Likewise, throughout the book that bears his name, Job bitterly questioned why the Lord was allowing his suffering and pain about as often as he affirmed his faith and trust in God. It was only later, when the Lord spoke to him at the end of his ordeal, that Job was able to give up his anger at God and trust in His sovereignty and love for him.

The prophet Elijah provides one of the most incredible instances of animosity toward God in 1 Kings 19. After receiving a death threat, Elijah became so stressed and upset that he fled and asked the Lord to take his life. Elijah was mad at God because he felt the Lord had abandoned him as a prophet. He told God, "I have been very zealous for the Lord God of hosts; for the children of Israel have forsaken Your covenant, torn down Your altars, and killed Your prophets with the sword. I alone am left; and they seek to take my life." (1 Kings 19:14, NKJV) Elijah remained disillusioned and angry at the Lord until God showed him that he was not alone, but there were still many others who were following Him. God gave Elijah specific directives that resulted in the deaths of Elijah's accusers, judgment for those who had turned their backs on God, and the training of Elisha to take Elijah's place as prophet upon Elijah's death (1 Kings 19:15-16; 2 Kings 2:1-11). In all of this, Elijah was never given a moment where he could exclaim, "Wow, you're so right, God. I'm going to change my attitude. I love you, Lord!" Instead, Elijah simply remained faithful in his actions as evidence that he trusted in God and His sovereignty, even when he wasn't provided an explanation for what was happening.

Animosity toward God is all too common with people I've counseled because many of them are in denial. At first, they don't think they're actually bitter at the Lord because they've convinced themselves that they are good Christians who don't doubt God's plans. But when I ask if they can trust God with their pain or trauma, they reply, "How can I? Look at what God has allowed. I'm afraid He is going to do something worse to me." Even if they're not outwardly angry at God, they clearly have bitterness toward Him and can't trust Him with what is going on in their lives. Yet it's when we start to trust that God will do what *is* best, not necessarily what we *think* is best, that we can start letting go of our animosity and experience peace.

It is very challenging to decide to unclench our fists and really trust God with our lives, no matter what He chooses to do with it. In the book *The Scars That Have Shaped Me*, Vaneetha Risner wrote about the story in the book of Daniel where Shadrach, Meshach, and Abednego faced capital punishment for refusing to worship a golden statue.

"In the Bible, Shadrach, Meshach, and Abednego were not guaranteed deliverance. Just before Nebuchadnezzar delivered them to the fire, they offered some of the most courageous words ever spoken. 'If we are thrown into the blazing furnace, the God we serve is able to deliver us from it ... But even if He does not, we want you to know... that we will not serve your gods.' (Daniel 3:17-18) Even if the worst happens, God's grace is sufficient. Those three young men faced the fire without fear because they knew that no matter the outcome, it would ultimately be for their good and God's glory. They did not ask what if the worst happened. They were satisfied knowing that even if the worst happened, God would take care of them. 'Even if.' Those two simple words can take the fear out of life. Replacing 'what if' with 'even if' in our mental vocabulary is one of the most liberating exchanges we can ever make. We trade our irrational fears of an uncertain future for the loving assurance of an unchanging God. We see that even if the very worst happens, God will carry us. He will still be good. And He will never leave us."[viii]

Peace through worship

The ability to say "even if" in all of your circumstances doesn't come from having control of them. It comes from an acknowledgment that you are out of control but trust in God's sovereignty. The only way that you will be able to give God that authority in your life is to grow in your adoration and love for God Himself. Shadrach, Meshach, and Abednego admitted they had no idea if God would actually save them. They even seemed to accept the very real possibility that He would let them die. But they had learned to value God so supremely that even if they lost what was most valuable to them, glorifying God, even to the bitter end, was worthy of their lives.

This is why Paul could write in Philippians 4:6, "Be anxious for nothing, but in everything by prayer and supplication, with thanksgiving, let your requests be made known to God." (NKJV) As alluded to earlier, some Christians have falsely interpreted this passage to mean that if we thank God no matter the circumstances, He will surely bless us, as if it's a formula to get our desired outcome from the Lord. That's actually the exact opposite of what Paul is teaching here. The reason we bring our prayers and desires to God with thanksgiving is not so we can get what we want from God, but so we can find peace in knowing that God is sufficient for us *regardless* of the outcome. Worship for the Christian is not just something done through singing in church. Worship is intended to be far more that that—a daily act of the will and heart to see and enjoy the supreme worth of God. The worship songs sung in church are certainly expressions of God's worth in our lives, but they are not to be the only way we worship Him.

Truth is, it is unnatural to be thankful to God and to see His beauty. It is much more inherent for us to be thankless toward God and completely focused on the things in front of us. Yet Psalm 103:1 exhorts us to, "Bless the Lord, O my soul; And all that is within me, bless His holy name!" (NKJV) When David wrote this, his soul was not wanting to praise God. Instead, he argued with his soul and forced himself to focus on God's goodness so that he could enjoy God and praise Him. David didn't do this because he had to. He wanted to worship God with all of his being because, while he didn't feel like it at that moment, he knew that God was supremely worthy and desired to experience God's worth. David was trying to push himself to praise God, recognizing that God is praiseworthy and good, even if he wasn't seeing it at that moment. He had seen it in the past, and because of that, David desired to stir himself up to experience God's goodness in a new and fresh way so he could praise Him and consummate that experience. That's also why David prayed to the Lord instead of trying to worship Him in his own strength. Genuine worship cannot be manufactured merely through force of will. If we praise God only because we know that we should, that isn't worship but hypocrisy. Authentic praise only comes through a genuine experience of our enjoyment of Him.

I was moved to understand the meaning of genuine worship and the value of experiencing God's worth most by the incredible C.S. Lewis. In his book *Reflections on the Psalms*, Lewis teaches that when we praise something, we're not just mouthing platitudes or saying it back, but we're actually in the midst of experiencing its goodness, and praise completes that experience. I liken it to how when we hear a funny joke, we laugh as a result. That laughter is praise. We are giving that joke the worth that it is due. But as we laugh, that laughter makes us enjoy and appreciate its worth even more.

Read carefully as Lewis elaborates:

"The most obvious fact about praise—whether of God or anything—strangely escaped me. I thought of it in terms of compliment, approval, or the giving of honour. I had never noticed that all enjoyment spontaneously overflows into praise unless … shyness or the fear of boring others is deliberately brought in to check it. The world rings with praise—lovers praising their mistresses, readers their favourite poet, walkers praising the countryside, players praising their favourite game—praise of weather, wines, dishes, actors, motors, horses, colleges, countries, historical personages, children, flowers, mountains, rare stamps, rare beetles, even sometimes politicians or scholars. I had not noticed how the humblest, and at the same time most balanced and capacious minds, praised most, while the cranks, misfits, and malcontents praised least ... Except where intolerably adverse circumstances interfere, praise almost seems to be inner health made audible … I had not noticed either that just as men spontaneously praise whatever they value, so they spontaneously urge us to join them in praising it: 'Isn't she lovely? Wasn't it glorious? Don't you think that magnificent?' The Psalmists in telling everyone to praise God are doing what all men do when they speak of what they care about. My whole, more general, difficulty about the praise of God depended on my absurdly denying to us, as regards the supremely Valuable, what we delight to do, what we indeed can't help doing, about everything else we value."

Lewis concludes, "I think we delight to praise what we enjoy because the praise not merely expresses but completes the enjoyment; it is its appointed consummation. It is not out of compliment that lovers keep on telling one another how beautiful they are; the delight is incomplete till it is expressed … If it were possible for a created soul fully … to 'appreciate,' that is to love and delight in, the worthiest object of all, and simultaneously at every moment to give this delight perfect expression, then that soul would be in supreme beautitude … The Scotch catechism says that man's chief end is 'to glorify God and enjoy Him forever.' But we shall then know that these are the same thing. Fully to enjoy is to glorify. In commanding us to glorify Him, God is inviting us to enjoy Him."[ix]

No wonder Psalm 90:14 says of God, "Satisfy us in the morning with your unfailing love, that we may sing for joy and be glad all our days." (NIV) These psalmists wanted to genuinely worship their God. They didn't want to just say great things about Him. They longed to experience His greatness firsthand and then praise Him sincerely from the deepest parts of their souls. We shouldn't try to make worship happen. Instead, we need to pray like these psalmists and ask the Lord to help us encounter and understand His glory in profound ways each and every day, something only He can do for us.

As we pray for God to show us His glory, we need to focus our minds to see His glory where it is most visible. We do this by searching His Word and seeking to see His beauty as we study His character. We also need to spend time thinking through our own lives, looking for ways God has been faithful to us and genuinely praising Him for that faithfulness. Then our worship won't be forced, but it will be an expression of enjoyment of our God.

Psalm 34:8 declares, "Oh, taste and see that the Lord is good; Blessed is the man who trusts in Him!" (NKJV) Worship for the Christian is not to be some heartless religious act done because God demands it. Instead, it is to be an act aimed at changing our hearts in order to see God as being supremely worthy and valuable in all areas of our lives—because He is.

A powerful example of this is seen in the life of the prophet Habakkuk. After my first deployment, I saw a level of violence and wickedness in Afghanistan that I had never witnessed before. I am not simply talking about the horrors I saw in firefights with the Taliban, but the day-to-day evil that the people of Marjah endured at the hands of this brutal gang of religious zealots. I came home filled with fear and anger over what I had seen, and it was then that God led me to read the book of Habakkuk.

It is a short and obscure book in the Old Testament written by a man who was witnessing constant evil in his society. At the beginning of the book, Habakkuk comes to the Lord and expresses incredible amounts of frustration toward God over what he was seeing. In response, God showed Habakkuk His plan to judge Israel through an even more violent and oppressive nation. Habakkuk's feelings of anger quickly shifted to fear as he realized that God's plans were far more devastating than he wanted. However, by the end of the book, Habakkuk had made his peace with God's plans. That peace didn't come from his understanding of why God was doing what He was, nor did it come through a lengthy discussion with God. Instead, Habakkuk's peace was birthed through worship.

The last chapter of the book is a song of praise to God written by Habakkuk that ends like this: "Though the fig tree may not blossom, Nor fruit be on the vines; Though the labor of the olive may fail, And the fields yield no food; Though the flock may be cut off from the fold, And there be no herd in the stalls—Yet I will rejoice in the Lord, I will joy in the God of my salvation. The Lord God is my strength; He will make my feet like deer's feet, and He will make me walk on my high hills." (Habakkuk 3:17-19, NKJV) Habakkuk began his prayer by acknowledging that his fears were going to come to pass. All the sustenance and prosperity of Israel would eventually be cut off through the wrath of God. Yet Habakkuk declared that he was going to rejoice, not in his circumstances, but in God Himself.

As important as it is to learn how to pour out our fears before God, if our eyes are never raised above our circumstances through the act of worship, our fears will always control us. Whatever is most important to us, and whatever has the most worth in our lives, will always capture our attention. If our attention is always on this world, which is so chaotic and beyond our control, then we will never be able to overcome our anxiety. But if our attention is on God, then we can rest and be thankful regardless of our circumstances and no matter how much fear we are feeling at the moment.

This won't be done overnight. It is a lifelong exercise. We need to learn the discipline to go to God every day with our fears. Through the act of pouring out our hearts to the Lord and training ourselves to worship Him above all else, God will meet us and increase our genuine enjoyment and praise of Him. As this happens, we will be able to accept His peace more and trust Him with our future.

Peace isn't an absence of fear, but courage and assurance in the midst of it. Remember, Jesus Himself was filled with such fear of the cross that He sweat blood in the Garden of Gethsemane (Luke 22:44). But even in the midst of those overwhelming fears, Jesus didn't find peace in stoically accepting His fate. Instead, He expressed His most heartfelt desire to His Father, knowing that He heard Him and would do what was best for Him. "If it is Your will, take this cup away from Me; nevertheless not My will, but Yours, be done." (Luke 22:42, NKJV) Christ prayed so long in Gethsemane that His disciples fell asleep three times. That means that in His time of greatest fear, Jesus poured out His heart to His Father not just once, but over and over again. That enabled Him to find comfort and peace in the midst of His fear.

We need to learn how to do this as Jesus did, offering our most heartfelt desires to God, not in an expectation that He will respond exactly as we desire, but with open hands, trusting our Father's will above our own because we know He hears us with sincere concern and care for our circumstances. God might answer our prayers the way we want, or His will may not line up with ours. Either way, we learn how to let go and trust that God will do what is best, even if that means we'll suffer what we most fear. We can do this only if we trust not in a particular outcome, but in the beautiful character of our wonderful Lord. As we begin to accept what has happened to us in the past and trust God with our future, we will experience more healing in our present.

When my wife and I experienced the miscarriage of our first child, we were terribly afraid of trying again. The only thing that gave us any peace at all was praying, "God, whatever you have for us, we want to accept it. We trust what you are going to do." When Emma became pregnant once again, there was a part of both of us that didn't want to believe that the child would come to term, mostly because we didn't want to be hurt again. But we determined together as a couple that in whatever amount of time God gave us with our child—a few days, a few months, whatever it was—we wanted to look back and be thankful for it, even if that time was only while the baby was in Emma's womb.

Our child, Fira (the name of an island in Greece that is also the Greek word for "lady"), was born in 2020, and it was our ability to pray, "Not my will, but yours" that got us through the intense fears of the pregnancy and continues to carry us onward today as young parents.

The Serenity Prayer
God, grant me the serenity to accept the things I cannot change, courage to change the things I can, and wisdom to know the difference. Living one day at a time, enjoying one moment at a time, accepting hardships as the pathway to peace; taking, as He did, this sinful world as it is, not as I would have it, trusting that He will make all things right if I surrender to His will; that I may be reasonably happy in this life and supremely happy with Him forever in the next. Amen.

We should pray this every day, not as a mindless mantra, but as something we spend time reflecting upon and even journaling about, while bringing our fears before God. Ask yourself, "What are those things in my life I cannot change?" "What are the specific fears about my past, present, and future that I can ask God to grant me the serenity to accept?" "How can I affirm that He is in control and will do what is best for me?" We can allow God to free us from all the pointless stress and worry about things that we have no ability to control in the first place. After all, Matthew 6:27 asks, "Can all your worries add a single moment to your life?" (NLT)

Once we do this, we can then move on to the things that we *can* change. There is much we can do something about in our lives. We need to list them and ask God for the courage to work on them, push forward into the unknown, and not remain paralyzed by fear. That allows us to then pray for the "wisdom to know the difference" and discover that many of the things we thought were in our control are actually not, while other things that we were too immobilized to work on are actually the very things that we should be addressing.

This part of the prayer is the most difficult to pray because when we try to balance giving up control in some areas and seeking to act in others, our fear will fight back. When this anxiety rears its ugly head, we automatically initiate mental and physical rituals to make it go away. As we do, our stress can build and become so strong, it feels unbearable. But we must fight it. Otherwise, our lives will be dictated by our fear.

For instance, let's say you struggle with a constant fear that your house will burn down. Every day before you leave home, you meticulously check all the electrical outlets and the burners on the stove to make sure everything is turned off properly. That ritual, in and of itself, isn't a bad thing, but over time the habit can become an obsession. Even when you know you haven't used the stove or plugged anything into the outlets, you still anxiously go around the house once, twice, then triple or even quadruple checking the house before leaving. When you try to stop this ritual, you feel panicked about it.

Your fear of a house fire has become overwhelming. You began the ritual as a means to feel in control and abate your anxiety. But that habit unwittingly became the source of your peace, so the more you did it, the more power you gave the fear over your thoughts and actions.

The same dynamic is true for the veteran at a restaurant who has to sit where he can see the door, the hypochondriac who has to look up every symptom they feel, the jealous spouse who incessantly checks their partner's email and social media, or the person who constantly seeks reassurance because they fear abandonment. Some of us spend hours at a time trapped in our own minds, obsessively reviewing our fears and insecurities, as if thinking about them will somehow make them go away. This not only plays itself out in what we do, but sometimes in what we refuse to do. Some of us give into fear by avoiding certain situations or environments because they're too stressful.

What can we do about obsessive fear? We can begin taking the time to weigh our thoughts, motives, and actions in order to see if we are being led by fear or by wisdom. Next, we need to realize that feeding an emotion will always make it bigger over time. So, as difficult and scary as it is, we must fight our fears, renew our minds, and even stop performing the rituals so that our fears won't continue to grow.

We begin this long and arduous journey by expressing our fears to God and learning to balance the acceptance of the things we cannot change with the courage to change the things we can. As we do this, we can then progress to sharing those fears with close friends and family, allowing them to help us better see the things we are doing that may be growing our fears. That allows us to confront our fears by slowly and intentionally coming against the promptings of our anxieties, recognizing the lies our emotions are telling us, and fighting those thoughts in the safety of God's presence.

At that point, we pray through the rest, remembering that what we want most is to be present with those we love. We don't want to spend our lives trapped in the past or worried about the future. We need to take each day one day at a time, knowing that hardships will come and God will turn them into "a far more exceeding and eternal weight of glory" (2 Corinthians 4:17), some sort of majesty, splendor, or honor for us now on earth or in the future in heaven, if we allow Him to do so. After all, if we don't see our suffering as something that God can use, but only view it as shameful, embarrassing, or even meaningless, then we can't receive the glory that God intends to produce for us.

Finally, we need to call to mind the promise of our Lord—that this world is not all that there is, and that we have wonderful hope in Him to redeem all of our brokenness and heal all of our wounds when we someday meet Him face to face. This world is not our ultimate home, but if we treat it like it is, we will be consumed with the fears and worries it holds.

Odd as it may seem, I felt far less stressed when I was deployed in the military than I did at home. A big part of that had to do with the fact that I felt more in control of my life in Afghanistan than ever before. In the States, our higher ups were always breathing down our necks and micromanaging our every move. We couldn't do anything unless we first ran it up an endless chain of command to get approval. Yet when I was fighting, we went out on patrol in small groups that we trusted, and we had almost complete autonomy to complete the mission as we saw fit. This was liberating at the time, but looking back now, I realize it wasn't good for me at all. It caused me to believe I had to be *more* in control of my actions, which made me grow to despise leadership and become more arrogant. This is one reason why so many military veterans struggle with authority, have severe control issues, and often yearn to return to combat zones.

On the positive side, being deployed and facing death began giving me a perspective to understand what was really important in life. Ecclesiastes 5:12 says, "The sleep of a laboring man is sweet, whether he eats little or much; but the abundance of the rich will not permit him sleep." (NKJV) In America, many perceive that an increase in prosperity will lead to a decrease in stress. We believe that getting that amazing career or having a certain amount of funds in our bank accounts will lead to a stress-free life, but in this Bible passage, the writer, King Solomon, saw the opposite as being true. It seemed to him that the wealthier a man was, the less he was able to rest or find peace.

I found this to be the case as well. It is amazing how many things there are to worry about when we live in a peacetime environment. Our job, our appearance, our relationships, and our health are just a few of the concerns. When I was in Afghanistan, though, these matters seemed petty in comparison to simple survival. I was in a life or death situation every day, but I actually felt at ease. I never overanalyzed physical problems or worried about germs or sickness. I was merely happy to be alive. I never stressed about relationships but was simply thankful I had relationships at all. I never complained about food, or any other luxury, because I was thankful to have anything at all. I never worried about finances but was just grateful I had finances to go back to. Plus, the people living in Afghanistan didn't have bank accounts, steady paychecks, 401(k)s, home decor, shopping malls, doctors, vacations, electricity, running water, or any of the other things we as Americans stress about or take for granted on a daily basis, yet they were content without them. No wonder, in spite of all our prosperity, Americans are the most stressed out people on earth. As luxury increases, so does our stress over things that are ultimately insignificant.

What we see at the end of the Serenity Prayer is the *eternal* perspective. This life isn't all there is, and as long as we can be "reasonably happy" in this life, we should be content knowing that there is an eternal life yet to come that is far more valuable. When we live this life like it's all there is, we can become incredibly anxious over objectively foolish things. We can't see the big picture, so we stress about every little, inconsequential detail. It's not that the things we worry about don't matter at all. It's just that, in the grand scheme of things, we often place ultimate stress on things that aren't that important.

Because of this, we have forgotten how to be thankful for the little things. We have forgotten to put ultimate stress on things that really matter, like our relationships—and especially the one we have with God. We can grow complacent in our relationship with the Lord, and we can become overly critical in our relationships with others. If we spent even a small amount of time thinking about the relationships that we have allowed to fall by the wayside or the fights that we have with our loved ones, we would feel pretty ashamed. When we finish praying the Serenity Prayer, our perspective should be to ask God to help us see the things that are most important so we can grow in peace and put first things first—to "number our days, that we may gain a heart of wisdom." (Psalm 90:12, NKJV)

Sometimes you can feel alone in your fears, like you are trapped in your own mind. When this happens, it is possible to become bitter toward those around you because they don't seem to take things as seriously as you do. In these moments, just saying your fears out loud can have tremendous power in helping to release you from them. I liken it to waking up from a dream. When you are dreaming, everything seems so rational, like it all makes sense. But the second you wake up, you realize just how ridiculous the dream really was. In the same way, when you tell others about your fears, the act of speaking tears away the illusion so you can see how irrational they are. Other people can also pray for your serenity, asking God to bring peace to your troubled and anxious mind. Even when you confess fears that are rational, you can listen as others give practical wisdom that will help you make the right decisions and calibrate your stress levels accordingly.

Fear doesn't have to isolate you. It can actually bring greater intimacy with those around you when you find the courage to talk about your fears in humility. That means you can't simply vent your fears to those around you, pouring them out and then, when you don't get the advice you want from others, ridicule or reject them. That isn't humility, but abuse that will push people away. But, if we can let them know in advance how we can sometimes be overcome by anxiety when we share our fears with them, then when we do vent and react poorly to their response, we can improve our communication with them and increase the likelihood of hearing, applying, and expressing our appreciation for their help.

Remember, while God can take whatever you share with Him because He already knows what is in your heart, your friends and family are different. Therefore, express your fears to God first and allow Him to help you calm down and understand things better. That will help you get into the right mindset so that when you do talk to those who are trying to help you, you can be quick to listen, slow to speak, and less likely to get angry (James 1:19). Be patient with them, knowing they won't always give you perfect advice, but thankful they are there for you because they care for you and are praying for you.

I share much more about our emotions in my book, *Rooted In Sin, Rescued By Love*—but just know that dealing with fear and growing in peace will change your life, and it will position you for healing. Find comfort in the perspective brought from this message and poem called "The Preacher and the Rose" and "Unfolding The Rosebud," as shared by Pastor Darryl Brown Jr., an author, motivational speaker, health educator, spiritual life coach, and founding and senior pastor of Kingdom Builders Christian Center in Omaha, Nebraska.

A new minister was walking with an older, more seasoned minister in the garden one day. Feeling a bit insecure about what God had for him to do, he was asking the older preacher for some advice. The older preacher walked up to a rosebush, handed the young preacher a rosebud, and told him to open it without tearing off any of the petals.

The young preacher looked in disbelief at the older preacher and was trying to figure out what a rosebud could possibly have to do with his wanting to know the will of God for his life and ministry. But, because of his great respect for the older preacher, he proceeded to try to unfold the rose while keeping every petal intact. It wasn't long before he realized how impossible this was to do.

Noticing the younger preacher's inability to unfold the rosebud without tearing it, the older preacher began to recite the following poem:

It is only a tiny rosebud,
A flower of God's design;
But I cannot unfold the petals
With these clumsy hands of mine.
The secret of unfolding flowers
Is not known to such as I.
God opens this flower so easily,
But in my hands they die.
If I cannot unfold a rosebud,
This flower of God's design,
Then how can I have the wisdom
To unfold this life of mine?
So, I'll trust in God for leading
Each moment of my day.
I will look to God for guidance
In each step along the way.
The path that lies before me,
Only my Lord and Savior knows.
I'll trust God to unfold the moments,
Just as He unfolds the rose.

Chapter 9
When We Can't Find the Words

There will be some of us, however, who won't be able to walk through this process of healing—not because we are unwilling, but because no matter how hard we try, we are unable to find the words to express what we are feeling.

This is something that impacts many people for a variety of reasons. Perhaps they were traumatized at an age where they didn't really understand what was happening. It could be that their pain was too extreme to be able to process. Maybe they spent so much time trying to suppress their trauma, they no longer know how to communicate it. Whatever the cause, when we are unable to process what we have been through, we won't be able to heal.

One such person was Amy who came from an emotionally abusive upbringing where her parents were very oppressive to her and her siblings. She took on the emotional responsibility for her younger brothers and sisters, and because of that, she was put in a situation where she suppressed her emotions instead of dealing with them. She had to be strong for her siblings, but that disabled her from being able to really understand what she was feeling and why she was feeling it. Anxiety punctuated by intense amounts of depression, regret, anger, fear, and worry made her feel like all of them were compounding upon her at once. For years, this literally locked her up psychologically and emotionally.

Throughout this book, I have gone over the importance of praying to God and asking Him to help you express and process what you have been through. This is a slow process as He gradually reveals your trauma to you through His Spirit, contemplation, and helpful counselors. In my experience, this is effective because of how gradual it is. Yet there are those who have been really patient with this process, but still can't find the words to express their trauma and its effect on them.

There is hope! A number of therapies have been developed that are worthy of consideration, such as Eye Movement Desensitization and Reprocessing (EMDR). EMDR is a psychotherapy treatment designed to alleviate the distress associated with traumatic memories. Successful treatments result in the relief of the distress, the reformulation of negative beliefs, and a reduction of the physiological arousal from that trauma.[x] I know people who have used this therapy and experienced amazing progress through it. Amy was one of them. Another was Rory. He grew up in a demented household where he was physically and sexually abused by his own father. That trauma held him back and held him down emotionally and physically until EMDR therapy gave him the ability to process his past trauma and move on to a healthy, positive future. Likewise, when Melody's mother died when she was very young, it produced in her feelings of abandonment that she couldn't really categorize or express when she later had a child of her own. The fear of losing her baby or of leaving her baby alone put Melody in a position where she couldn't function. EMDR therapy helped her so that she could function and become a happy, nurturing mother.

Another option is art therapy. Art, unlike other modes of expression, doesn't require full understanding to appreciate. Instead, art passes over the language center of the brain and enables someone to express something directly from their heart, often without using words. Even with art like poetry that does require words, there is still something in that which enables someone to articulate the inexpressible because they are able to use metaphor and symbolism to express something that was previously beyond their comprehension.

Simply put, an art therapist encourages expression utilizing artistic means: paint, music, writing, and so on. These therapists allow their patients to either view, hear, or create art in order to help them discern their trauma. For instance, they might ask a patient to paint a picture of a storm or to paint on a mask. As the patient creates, the therapist will walk them through the subconscious choices they made in making their painting, such as the colors they used or the subtle techniques they employed with their brushes. They might have a patient listen to classical symphonies and walk them through the emotions being conveyed in the music to help them understand the feelings present in themselves. As they delve into the art, they can discover and express things trapped in the subconscious part of the brain that they were previously unable to apprehend. When our emotions get blocked up and have no outlet, art can get us unblocked and enable us to understand and convey our emotions.

Art therapy is found in the Bible through the wealth of poems and songs written by the saints of old that helped them express and deal with their internal wounds. Even King Saul had a "distressing spirit" in 1 Samuel 16:14-23, and it was only through hearing David play the harp that he experienced rest and refreshment. God created all forms and fashions of artistic expression, and they seem to not only have a pleasing effect, but a therapeutic one as well.

As I've mentioned previously, Psalm 42 is my absolute favorite Psalm in Scripture because it deals with the difficult topics of grief and depression. For most of my life, I have struggled with depression and didn't know how to express what was going on inside of me. I knew that I naturally gravitated toward depressing movies and music, but I never understood why and, therefore, I never found any relief. Then I read Psalm 42:7. "Deep calls unto deep at the noise of Your waterfalls; All Your waves and billows have gone over me." (NKJV) Reading those words for the first time unblocked something within me. It gave expression to something that I previously lacked the words to articulate.

The psalmist poetically expresses what it is like to be depressed. The first metaphor he uses is a waterfall. When we look at a waterfall, we see a constant torrent of water bearing down on the rocks below, slowly eroding them under its immense force. This was one aspect of my depression. It felt like a constant force bearing down on me, eating away at my emotional and physical vitality non-stop for days, weeks, or even months at a time.

But then the psalmist switches to the metaphor of "waves and billows" crashing over him. If you have ever gone to the beach and had a wave crash over your head, you know exactly what he is talking about. Sometimes depression isn't like a constant pressure eroding our energy; instead, it comes in sudden, violent oppression. When going through a season of grief or depression, there will be times when I feel fine and am experiencing no sadness, only to unexpectedly get hit with a massive wave of emotion. It will sweep me off my feet and completely disorient me. For a time that feels like an eternity, the emotion will be so powerful that it's almost like being underwater, desperate for oxygen. Then, as suddenly as it came, it leaves. This process of getting hit by wave after wave of surging emotion makes me feel anxious and always on guard for the next onslaught.

Those words, written by a man who lived almost 3,000 years before me, gave me the words that I lacked to describe what I was going through—and a deep fellowship with someone I had never met. I no longer felt alone in my emotions but knew there was at least one other person who felt what I felt and understood where I was coming from. When we lack the words to describe our emotional state, we can become frustrated with ourselves and even feel stupid, giving up on trying to talk about what we are feeling. This increases our isolation from others and deepens our wounds as we never try to tend it or heal from it. But when we find the words, we gain the ability and courage to then express our feelings to those around us and grow in healing and unity with them and God.

I have also benefitted from art therapy received through motion pictures. The movie *Inception,* starring Leonardo DiCaprio, mainly deals with the concept of people discovering technology that enables them to go into another person's dreams. At the beginning of the movie, we meet a man named Cobb who is haunted by his past mistakes. At one point, we learn that Cobb has used this technology to construct a "hotel" filled with his greatest regrets. Every time he slept, he would go through each floor of this hotel and experience another moment that he regretted in hopes that he could somehow alter his past failures. But when Cobb begins dreaming, he realizes he is unable to change his past and so remains trapped in his mind, completely helpless to affect his haunting past.

That metaphor was so powerful to me. It helped me to grasp what it was like to be trapped in my own head, consumed by regret. It helped me to once again recognize that I wasn't alone, and that ruminating over my past was not going to help me heal from it. Being imprisoned in my past made me unable to enjoy my present. It also showed me that while I couldn't change my past, I could learn from it and build a better future. A rap music artist named NF uses this same metaphor in a song he wrote entitled, "Mansion." He uses it to describe being trapped in his own mind, reliving his past over and over again as he visits all the "rooms" of his broken past. He does this in an attempt to cope with his pain, but he finds that all this does is isolate him and keep him incarcerated.

Even J.R.R. Tolkien, who I quoted at the beginning of this book, used his art form to express his pain. A lot of what you find in *The Lord of the Rings* was inspired by his horrible experiences in World War I. When he described the desolate wastelands of Mordor that contained no vegetation or life, toxic fumes that were constantly in the air, smoke and brimstone always erupting from Mount Doom, and the constant, unending waves of Orcs, he was using metaphor in order to express what it was like to be in the trenches during the war. He was able to use Middle-earth to understand for himself the pain that he was experiencing in his own heart.

The power of artistic expression is evident. It is a universal language spoken by all people for all time. Art is a mighty tool that can be used by God to genuinely help you understand and process things that were previously beyond your ability. This, in turn, will give you the words and the fellowship you need to begin healing from what has happened to you.

Of course, each one of us is unique. We cannot expect any therapy to be a cookie-cutter solution to addressing our trauma. However, with prayer and trusted consultation, EMDR, art, and other therapeutic approaches can be effective and are worthy of your consideration.

Consistency in healing

I am still learning about healing, and there are times when I forget the truths I am sharing with you. It isn't enough to have a moment of clarity. You need to walk daily through life and deal with your emotional trauma as it comes up. Whenever you are triggered and overreact to a situation, you should reflect on what you did and why you did it. Our emotional triggers and extreme reactions are great indicators of what is still broken in us and needs to be worked on and healed. Take some time to journal or simply meditate, asking yourself, "Before I overreacted, what was I feeling?" "Why was I feeling that?" "How did I react to that emotion?" "Why did I react that way?" "What is it, from my past, that caused that reaction?"

Then, as you ask these questions, take them to God in prayer. If you were triggered by something that caused you to experience incredible sorrow, start pouring out your despair before God instead of suppressing it. Ask Him for comfort in your present sadness and healing from your past pain. If you experienced anxiety or stress, express that concern to God and ask for increased faith in Him and in what He is doing in your life. If you became angry, it could be there is an event or a person that you haven't fully forgiven. Take your rage to God again and ask Him to give you the strength to forgive. If you felt guilty, bring that sense of wrongdoing to God and ask for clarity to see if you need to receive more forgiveness for what you have done or acceptance that what happened wasn't your fault.

As annoying as your triggers might be, you have to start seeing them as opportunities to grow and seek increased insight about your past trauma that will bring increased healing in your present. Always keep in mind this is a long process and won't be over quickly. Don't expect to understand all of your emotions or to heal overnight. It might take years to fully comprehend what lies behind your emotions. But don't get discouraged as you wait or when you have setbacks. Unfortunately, you will experience seasons of growth and victory, completely unbothered by your past or your triggers, only to be met by an unexpected season where you are dragged right back into your trauma.

This is a normal part of the healing process—and these setbacks are calls to press in to God more than ever, trusting that He will walk you through it. Keep pouring out your heart to Him. Don't let your discouragement pull you from the resources that your Father has given you. He will provide grace to help you cope with your emotions in the present, and He who has begun this good work in you will be faithful to complete it (Philippians 1:6).

To maintain consistency in your healing, also be sure to confess your sins to God. Sometimes as Christians we can think that there is no need to confess because Jesus has died for us and all of our sins are forgiven. Yet when we sin against God, while we are indeed forgiven, there will be an awkwardness in our relationship with Him unless the sin is exposed and confessed. If you try to forget about your sins or act like they never happened, it will ultimately hurt your unity with God and hinder your ability to change your behavior and grow. This is why 1 John 1:9 tells us, "If we confess our sins, He is faithful and just to forgive us our sins and to cleanse us from all unrighteousness." (NKJV) Confession is vital and necessary.

Finally, it is important to ask God for the courage to humble ourselves and apologize for our behavior to the people affected by our overreactions to our emotional triggers. This was massively important for me, but insanely difficult to implement. Whenever I overreacted, I was really embarrassed about it, so I moved on and acted like it never took place. Covering over my behavior made me calloused and blind toward how bad my behavior actually was. But if I apologized for my behavior, simply saying out loud what I was sorry for, and even why I reacted that way, it gave me a great amount of insight into my behavior and made me that much more aware of my emotions.

The issue of pride
Regularly and persistently dealing with our trauma and seeking effective therapies when we struggle to express our trauma in words will humble us—and that is crucial. The Bible tells us that our main issue as human beings is not our past trauma or current bad behavior but our pride and self-reliance (James 4:1-6). In today's culture, we tend to make healing a selfish, almost narcissistic act where we are told to "love ourselves" or "forgive ourselves." While such well-meaning platitudes might help someone with their trauma, it can also make them even worse off than before as they become more self-centered and hardened toward their wrong behavior. Some who are hurting from trauma actually think everyone around them should just put up with their bad conduct and excuse them whenever they act out.

We need to see healing not as an outcome to make our self-absorbed lives better, but as an act of grace from God designed to make us more whole for His glory. As Ezekiel 36:22-23 declares, "Therefore say to the house of Israel, 'Thus says the Lord God: "I do not do this for your sake, O house of Israel, but for My holy name's sake, which you have profaned among the nations wherever you went. And I will sanctify My great name, which has been profaned among the nations, which you have profaned in their midst; and the nations shall know that I am the Lord," says the Lord God, "when I am hallowed in you before their eyes." (NKJV) God spoke these words to His people when He promised to save them from their captivity, and He wanted them to understand that He was acting for His own glory, not merely for their sake.

That may sound cold and unloving, but remember that the Lord is the greatest good in the universe, not us. If God healed me simply for my own sake, my eyes wouldn't be drawn to Him but to myself and my own needs. Yes, my trauma was bad, and it hurt me in many ways, but even without it, I am still a mess of a person who needs a Savior. God truly loves us and cares deeply about us and our healing—but it is precisely because God loves us and cares so much for us that He must take our eyes off of ourselves and elevate our hearts to be consumed with His supreme glory and satisfaction. If this never happens, while we might be less affected by our past trauma, we will become more selfish and distant from Him. That is not what we need.

Therefore, we have to constantly search ourselves and ask, "Am I coming to God merely for what He can do for me, or am I coming to Him because I love Him and want to be closer to Him?" If we come to God only for what He can do for us, then we will continue to be consumed with ourselves. Then, if we are healed, we will become far prouder and even more convinced that the reason why we are healed is because we must be mentally stronger and more resilient than the average person. We'll believe that we were able to overcome our past and take control of our future because *we* had the will and strategy to change.

That kind of thinking will only sink us deeper into self-denial about our struggles and issues, making us more likely to shift blame and ignore criticism because we feel we're always right and don't need to listen to others. That will take away our ability to have compassion or empathy for those around us. When they come to us for help, we'll just tell them to tough it out and overcome like we did. We'll become rude and brash, unable to genuinely care for others. Worst of all, we'll gain no unity with God through our healing. We might be happier and possibly even more religious than before, but there will be no authentic intimacy and joy in our relationship with God, which is the greatest good that we can ever hope to have.

If we fail to heal, or if our healing takes longer than we think it should, it will lead us to despair. When we have a setback or struggle with a trigger or negative emotion, we might even blame God and accuse Him of being a useless Savior. Yet Scripture says to "count it all joy when you fall into various trials, knowing that the testing of your faith produces patience. But let patience have its perfect work, that you may be perfect and complete, lacking nothing." (James 1:2-4, NKJV) Because biblical authors like James (the brother of Jesus) had such love for God and desire for Him, they had a very strange perspective on suffering and struggling against temptations and emotions. They didn't see their battles as God failing them, but as opportunities to draw closer to the Lord even though the trials themselves were painful and horrible.

Hebrews 12:2 takes it even further, exhorting us to look to "Jesus, the author and finisher of our faith, who for the joy that was set before Him endured the cross, despising the shame, and has sat down at the right hand of the throne of God." (NKJV) The cross certainly wasn't joyful in and of itself to Jesus. He despised the shame and the pain that He had to endure. But it was the result of the cross that brought Him joy, because when He suffered, it brought us near to Him.

When we struggle with healing in God, we need to remember that the ultimate goal is intimacy with Him, not freedom from our emotions. Even when we are hit with a trigger or a horrible negative emotion, while that is terrible and painful in and of itself, we can see the result of that emotion or temptation as an opportunity to press in to Jesus through our weakness, pain, and fear, so it can produce joy in our lives. If we can grow in our understanding of this principle, then our healing can't produce pride because our hearts will be so consumed with God and His glory that we will have nothing to be proud about. Rather, we will only find deep amounts of joy and thanks for Him. If our healing is going slower than we want, or if God chooses not to heal us completely, it won't bring despair. We'll still rely on Him more and have hope in Him.

The glory of God

As mentioned earlier in this book, the word "glory" in the Bible carries with it the idea of weight, importance, or majesty. So, the more we respect, honor, or "glory" someone, the more significance their words have on us. In John 10:27, Jesus declared, "My sheep hear My voice, and I know them, and they follow Me." (NKJV) Christ was saying that, in order to really follow Him, people had to consider themselves as being the same as lowly sheep who are trusting and following their shepherd. Sheep are relatively helpless animals. They don't have much capacity to fend for themselves, much less take care of their needs. They are completely dependent on the guidance of their shepherd.

If, as Christians, we are consumed with pride, we may hear and even know the words of our Savior, but they won't move us because they have no weight in our lives. We fail to glorify Him. Therefore, if we are reliant on ourselves in dealing with our trauma, then read that God has forgiven us, accepted us, and made us holy and blameless in His sight by His blood, we may not believe or honor it. We value our own voice over His. Over time, we discover that the only reason why we have any confidence at all is not because we're listening to the voice of our "good shepherd" (John 10:11), but because we're relying on our own puffed up opinion of ourselves.

That leaves us in a fragile state when it comes to overcoming our trauma. When we are struggling with fear and anxiety and hear that God tells us to trust in Him because He knows what is best for us and that no desire of His can be stopped (Job 42:2, Psalm 115:3), it doesn't give us peace because we trust in ourselves far more than in Him. When we read that He alone is our treasure and reward, so that if every desire of our lives should fail but we still gain Christ, we have all we need (Psalm 16:11, Psalm 73:25-26), we don't believe it. When we are crushed by sadness and Jesus comes to comfort us, we don't experience comfort because our love for God isn't deep enough to be truly consoled by Him. When we wrestle with anger, we can't find rest in forgiveness because we don't trust in the justice of God enough to let Him judge for us.

All of the rest, comfort, peace, joy, and healing that is offered by God can only be received by those who give God supreme glory in their lives. Your pride can literally keep you from experiencing the blessings of God. Unless your pursuit of healing is found in your pursuit of God's glory, you will not be able to have true healing in God. The more you love God, and the more you grow in your understanding and trust in Him, the more weight His Word will have on you. Then, even in the midst of your most extreme emotions from your trauma, you will stand firm because you will be held by the glory of your God!

The greatest thing God has done, and continues to do, for me is to show me that my life is not about me, but about Him. The more I lose sight of that, the more miserable I am and the more hurtful I am toward others, trauma or no trauma. But the more I confess my trauma to God and others, the more His mercy and forgiveness are available to bring genuine healing and growth in Him.

The truth is, we are all broken to some extent. Yet the more we open up, the more we can see that we have a commonality in brokenness. While everyone's brokenness is unique, we can help and support one another. We are not alone, and there are people around us who do care about us in our pain and will be with us in our struggles.

Bear one another's burdens, and so fulfill the law of Christ.
Galatians 6:2, NKJV

It is amazing to know that I have a relationship with my Savior, Jesus Christ, who fully understands me. He doesn't condemn me, but instead dwells with me (Romans 8:1-2) and helps me with my trauma and pain. This makes me more whole every day.

Yet as incredible as this is, it is also important for me to have relationships with others who can affirm these truths to me and aid me in understanding them better. I need a community around me to help me see that even when I feel alone, I'm not. If those around me can't exactly understand what I've been through, that doesn't mean they can't relate at all. Every one of us has pain and fears that we can share with one another—and it's when we see each other's brokenness and experience each other's care that we can finally stop feeling so alone and hopeless. We can work with one another to face our emotions and our pasts, and we can pray together that we might find healing from God. As James 5:16 tells us, "Confess your trespasses to one another, and pray for one another, that you may be healed. The effective, fervent prayer of a righteous man avails much." (NKJV)

Our emotions will tell us that our trauma isolates us from other people and makes us different. But the truth is, our trauma and pain actually have tremendous power to draw us closer together as we allow ourselves to empathize with one another. It's just as 2 Corinthians 1:3-4 says. "Blessed be the God and Father of our Lord Jesus Christ, the Father of mercies and God of all comfort, who comforts us in all our tribulation, that we may be able to comfort those who are in any trouble, with the comfort with which we ourselves are comforted by God." (NKJV)

If you are recovering from trauma, let me remind you once more that you aren't alone. That might be hard to believe because you may have taught yourself it is a weakness to need help, or you would feel like a burden to others to ask for it. But you have to understand that trauma, and the shame that accompanies it, thrives in the dark. The more you try to hide your past, the more your shame will root you in your trauma and the more your past will have power over you. It's when we cultivate community that we can safely bring our trauma into the light and watch our shame melt away.

God also wants us to share our healing with others. Now, if you are in the process of healing right now, don't get too far ahead of yourself and immediately go out looking to help others when you are still in the early stages of recovery. But as you become more and more restored, sharing your healing and seeking to aid others who are not as far along as you are can solidify God's curative work in your life and spur you to recover faster.

It is interesting that one of the therapies recommended to people with PTSD is working with horses. There are a number of reasons this helps, but one of the primary ones is that horses themselves can be traumatized and easily spooked. As someone works with these animals to help them cope with being agitated, it allows them to better understand and experience their own healing. It also provides the person with a sense of purpose because their healing is no longer only about them, but it is about the well-being of another creature as well. The old adage is certainly true: you will never understand something better than when you have to teach it. When you realize that God desires for you to show others the hope and comfort that He has shown you, your healing will grow in a much more dynamic way and produce even more unselfishness and humility in you.

What we need most as we process our trauma is people to be with us in our pain, offering encouragement when we are down, correction when our thinking is skewed, and comfort in our suffering. Others can also ask us searching questions like, "Why did you react like that?" "Is it something that I did or said?" "What is this event bringing up for you?" "What is this reminding you of?" It's also great to hear, "I forgive you and love you. How can I help you better deal with this in the future?" Our knee jerk reaction might be to get embarrassed and upset, but if our friends or family remain patient and determined to help us walk through our trauma, then when we are ready, they can be available to talk us through our pain and emotions. Remember, healing is a process. We mustn't try to rush it, but instead, we should pray for patience. In the end, it is love and fellowship that we need the most. We simply desire someone's consistent presence and care.

Why we don't heal
Those who have experienced trauma have to choose to walk through healing on their own. This might sound strange, but some people will actually reject healing and cling to their familiar coping mechanisms. They will be so comfortable and reliant on their coping crutches that the thought of giving them up will be too much. Some people, like me, will reject healing because they don't want to be vulnerable. They will see their anger and apathy as a strength and will keep themselves closed off so they are not perceived as being weak. There will even be people who are convinced they are too badly damaged to be made whole and won't even try.

Admitting that we are broken and that our behavior is unhealthy is a very humbling act. Because most of us want to see ourselves as being strong and whole, we'll refuse to recognize we are broken, and through that denial, we remain broken. Should someone so much as mention that we need help, we'll become defensive and angry. It's not unlike what Jesus faced when many refused to come to Him and receive salvation even though He had the power to give it to them. In John 8:31-36, "Jesus said to the Jews who had believed him, 'If you abide in my word, you are truly my disciples, and you will know the truth, and the truth will set you free.' They answered him, 'We are offspring of Abraham and have never been enslaved to anyone. How is it that you say, "You will become free"?' Jesus answered them, 'Truly, truly, I say to you, everyone who practices sin is a slave to sin. The slave does not remain in the house forever; the son remains forever. So if the Son sets you free, you will be free indeed.'" (ESV)

Christ offered true and real freedom, but pride stopped many from being able to admit that they were slaves in need of a Savior. They became angry at Jesus for even suggesting that they were in bondage. This level of denial happens when we, at some level, realize that we are not the people that we desire to be. Instead of admitting helplessness, we convince ourselves that we are whole when we are not. Jesus told them, and us, that it is truth that sets us free. The lies that we tell ourselves might bring superficial comfort, but they cannot set us free.

Then there are those who undermine their healing by becoming addicted to their victim status. They refuse healing because they feel a sick joy and superiority from excusing all their bad behavior and poor life choices by blaming it on their past trauma. It can feel good to be the outcast, the person with the sad backstory that no one can really understand, but can only feel sorry for. This has become an increasingly big problem in society today because, unfortunately, being a victim has become a coveted status that grants some a platform to be heard over others. People like this will be quick to make excuses for themselves, blame others, vent their emotions, and share their past, but they won't be able to listen to criticism or correction.

Proverbs 18:1-2 describes the person addicted to their victimization, saying that "a man who isolates himself seeks his own desire; He rages against all wise judgment. A fool has no delight in understanding, But in expressing his own heart." (NKJV) In reality, their pride will prevent them from healing. They will be blind to the damage they are doing to others, they will complain constantly to anyone who will hear them, but they won't listen to others when they share their own hurt, and they will reject any advice given to them.

Some who stay broken do so because they lack the commitment to follow through on their healing. They fail to realize that healing is a long process, so they will have several "breakthrough" moments followed by just as many severe relapses. True healing and change don't happen at one seminar or counseling session. One powerful moment of clarity doesn't mean healing is complete. Healing requires consistency and discipline. It isn't something you pursue until your symptoms go away for a time. It is something that you address until the roots of your problems are healed, and that usually requires years of diligent effort.

Finally, we must take an active role in our healing. Counseling and therapy is to be a gentle process that walks us through understanding our own psyche and pain as we are given mental and spiritual tools to address our issues. But this is just as much on the person being counseled as it is on the person doing the counseling. If we aren't taking the time to truly scrutinize the things we are discovering or applying what we are learning, we might have the best counselor and therapy possible, but we'll still not grow or heal. In addition, we cannot ignore good counsel simply because we don't like it. We should have a humble attitude, realizing that we don't know it all and that we need to learn from our sessions.

Be cautious and thoughtful of the counsel that you are receiving, give respect to your therapist, and scrutinize your own heart to make sure that you aren't being arrogant and closed off or mindlessly accepting everything you are being told. When the counsel is sound and biblical, submit to it and be diligent to practice it. Acts 17:11 exhorts, "These were more fair-minded than those in Thessalonica, in that they received the word with all readiness, and searched the Scriptures daily to find out whether these things were so." (NKJV)

Finally, for those friends and family members who know someone who is getting more and more violent, hurtful, manipulative, and self-destructive and are not sincerely seeking help or healing, distance is the best help you can give them. You can't force someone to get help, and you may even be allowing yourself to be abused and taken advantage of. It's not that you don't love them, but you might be enabling them. It is tragic that the victims of yesterday tend to be the monsters of today, and as sad as their story might be, you must not tolerate bad behavior simply because you feel bad for someone. What is best for that person is that they get help—and staying with them, excusing their behavior, and sticking up for them is likely preventing them from getting the help they need. It's up to them, and them alone, to be proactive in their healing, and if they don't, that is their responsibility, not yours. Keep praying for them, reminding yourself that you aren't capable of healing this person. While God can use us to help others, He alone is our healer, and they need to go to Him. If they start to genuinely make concrete steps forward in seeking help, apologizing, and making amends for what they have done, you can begin to re-enter their lives. But because healing takes time, wait for an appropriate period before fully reconciling—then be sure to keep them accountable so that they don't become lackadaisical or apathetic and stop seeking help.

In the end, as good as counseling and therapy is, it does not replace our need for genuine communion with others. We need to have community, love, and understanding. The good news is that everyone who genuinely invests in their healing process can recover and discover how to function within their pain. Some mental scars will be so deep that they won't ever truly go away, but even when that is the case, it doesn't mean that we can't grow and learn how to function better through our issues.

The most important thing is to not give up. The road to healing is long, and I am still on it —but every step forward is a step closer to wholeness, and we are promised that one day we will be in the presence of our God and we will be whole. As Paul wrote in Philippians 3:13-14, "No, dear brothers and sisters, I have not achieved it, but I focus on this one thing: Forgetting the past and looking forward to what lies ahead, I press on to reach the end of the race and receive the heavenly prize for which God, through Christ Jesus, is calling us." (NLT)

Beloved, now we are children of God; and it has not yet been revealed what we shall be, but we know that when He is revealed, we shall be like Him, for we shall see Him as He is. And everyone who has this hope in Him purifies himself, just as He is pure.
1 John 3:2-3, NKJV

Sources

[i] Dr. Courtney Warren TED Talk: https://www.youtube.com/watch?v=YpEeSa6zBTE. TED Conferences, LLC is an American media organization that posts talks online for free distribution under the slogan "ideas worth spreading."

[ii] See https://ourworldindata.org/mental-health#depression

[iii] Joni Eareckson Tada, Foreword to Choosing Gratitude: Your Journey To Joy by Nancy Leigh DeMoss (Chicago: Moody Publishers, 2009), Page 12.

[iv] Taken by the author from a transcription of the audio of a longer version of the sermon. "Loving Your Enemies," delivered at the Detroit Council of Churches' Noon Lenten Services. The Martin Luther King, Jr. Papers Project, March 7, 1961. See also: https://www.youtube.com/watch?v=522wcqUlS0Y

[v] Our story of rape and reconciliation. Thordis Elva and Tom Stranger. TED Talk: https://www.youtube.com/watch?v=gyPoqFcvt9w

[vi] Taken by the author from Dorothy L. Sayers' book: Creed or Chaos?: Why Christians Must Choose Either Dogma or Disaster; Or, Why It Really Does Matter What You Believe.

[vii] Andrew Solomon TED Talk: https://www.youtube.com/watch?v=-eBUcBfkVCo

[viii] Vaneetha Rendall Risner, The Scars That Have Shaped Me: How God Meets Us In Suffering (Published by Desiring God, 2016), Page 118. Kindle Edition.

[ix] C.S. Lewis, Reflections on the Psalms (New York: Harcourt, Brace & Co., 1958), Pages 93-97.

[x] The EMDR Institute, Inc. https://www.emdr.com/what-is-emdr/